FINANCIAL LITERACY

Ali M. Reza

Copyright © 2019 by Ali M. Reza

All rights reserved

The author has nearly fifty years of experience in investments and finance. He has taught economics, finance and investments at the University of California (Davis), the University of Pittsburgh, San Jose State University, and the Rouen Graduate School of Business (France), and has conducted seminars for executives.

FOREWORD

Investment and finance are complex fields and have become quite technical and mathematical. Many people have difficulty understanding finance and investment; this is true for even those with a college education. As a result, people often make poor financial and investment decisions, or makes them easy prey for deceitful people. There is no need for this state of affairs. Finance and investments are everybody's business.

This book is written in a nontechnical, conversational tone. Anyone with a college or high school education can follow the material in this book. Various topics and chapters can be omitted, depending on your experience and interests. Accordingly, the book can be read in as little as three or four hours.

This book is an excellent source for students who are currently taking courses in finance or investments. It provides a summary of various topics, using an intuitive approach. By reading the relevant material, the student can prepare herself or himself for the upcoming class lecture or better understand the material after the lecture has been delivered.

People working for organizations, private or public, will find this book useful since it provides the basic knowledge of financial and investment issues of concern to them. Such knowledge will enhance your ability to establish closer relationships with coworkers. Finally, small businesses will find topics that they can use to improve their business, and better communicate with and understand their financial consultants and sources.

Everyone, whether employed, running a business, or currently not in the labor force, can benefit from the content of this book. You can learn how to evaluate alternative financial possibilities; this includes identifying fraudulent bargains.

TABLE OF CONTENTS

Chapter 1. The Economy	1
Gross Domestic Product	1
Size of the U.S. Economy	4
GDP Composition	6
Economic Sectors	7
Business Cycles	9
Inflation	14
Chapter 2. The Financial System	17
The Financial System's Features	17
Primary Markets	19
Secondary Markets	20
Money Markets and Capital Markets	20
The U.S. Treasury Department	20
The Federal Reserve	21

Commercial Banks	24
Savings Institutions	26
Credit Unions	27
Finance Companies	28
Insurance Companies	29
Securities Firms and Investment Banks	30
Check Cashing Businesses and Loan Sharks	32
Chapter 3. Financial Markets: Efficient or Inefficient?	33
Chapter 4. Present Value, Future Value	37
One-Period Cash Flow	38
Multiperiod Uniform Cash Flows	42
Multiperiod Varying Cash Flows	46
Chapter 5. Income and Wealth	49
Income	49
Wealth	51

Chapter 6. Financial Accounting: 55

    Income Statement and Balance Sheet

    Earnings Per Share (EPS) 59

    P/E Ratio 60

    GAAP and Pro-forma Financial Statements 61

Chapter 7. Leverage 63

Chapter 8. Interest Rates, Dividends, and Rate of Return 69

    Interest Rate 69

    Negative Interest Rate 70

    Simple Interest 72

    Compound Interest 72

    Return on Investment 73

    Dividend 75

    Capital Gain 76

    Long Term and Short Term Interest Rates 77

Chapter 9. Risk and Return 79

What is Risk?	80
Types of Risk: Market and Specific	81
Compensation for Taking Risk	84
Benefits of Diversification	84
Alpha and Beta	86
Chapter 10. Securities	**89**
Real Assets and Financial Assets	89
Economic Efficiency of Financial Assets and Markets	90
Securities Regulations	94
Chapter 11. Stocks	**96**
Stock Market	97
Stock Market Indexes	98
Common Stocks, Preferred Stocks	100
Return to Stocks	101
Predictability of Stock Prices and Returns	104
Stock Valuation	109

Risk as a Factor Determining Stock Returns	111
Price-Earnings Ratio	112
Business Success and Stock Performance	116
Outstanding Fund Managers and Forecasters	117
How to Ensure to Invest in the "Right" Stocks	120
Mechanics of Investing in Securities	121
Buying on Margin, Selling Short	123
Day Trading	124
Chapter 12. Bonds	**127**
Liquidity of Bonds and Price Effect	132
Attributes of Bonds	133
Different Types of Bonds	137
Treasury Bills Return versus Inflation	141
Connection Between Long Term and Short Term Interest Rates	143
Yield Inversion	144

Chapter 13. Collectibles, Art Work and Antiques	146
Chapter 14. Precious Metals and Cryptocurrencies	154
Precious Metals	154
Cryptocurrencies	158
Chapter 15. Real Estate	159
Chapter 16. Derivatives: Options, Warrants, Forwards/Futures, Swap, and CDS	166
Options	166
Creation of Options	167
Option Example	169
Warrants	176
Forwards and Futures	177
Spot Price, Forward and Futures Prices	179
Credit Default Swaps (CDS)	179
Swaps	181
Chapter 17. Investment Vehicles	183

Mutual Funds	183
Exchange Traded Funds (ETF)	185
Closed-end Funds	188
Real Estate Investment Trusts (REIT)	189
Money Market Mutual Funds	189
Unit Investment Trusts	190
Hedge Funds	190
Private Equity	192
Venture Capital	193
Angel Investors	194
Crowd Funding	194
Pension Funds	195
Ponzi Schemes or Pyramids	197
Chapter 18. Human Capital	200
Earnings Time Profile	200
Education and Training	203

Professional Athletes (and Other Stars)	205
Human Capital versus Other Assets	208
Chapter 19. Stock Dividends, Stock Splits and Stock Buybacks	**209**
Cash Dividends and Value of Stocks	209
Stock Buybacks	211
Stock Dividends	212
Stock Splits	212
References	215
Index	217

Chapter 1

THE ECONOMY

Business and financial activities take place in the economy; it is therefore important for everyone, but especially for the investor, to be knowledgeable about the overall economy and some of the characteristics of the nation's business and financial institutions. This section reviews some of the essential features of the U.S. economy. Later sections will consider the other attributes.

Gross Domestic Product: GDP

There are various measures one can use to measure the size of an economy. One is its population; another is the number of people who work, the size of its labor force. For the U.S., they are 327 million and 327 million, respectively. Here the focus is on the income the economy generates.

The starting point is the *Gross Domestic Product*, the *GDP*. This reflects the market value of everything Americans produce during a given time period. The GDP measures everything that goes through the market, that is, goods and services that are bought and sold. This means that if you paint your house yourself, the value of your labor does not show up in the

GDP. But if you pay someone $3,000 to paint it for you, GDP goes up by $3,000. Until a few years ago many women stayed at home to clean, cook and babysit; the value of this work was not reflected in GDP. Consider what happens if Ms A goes to Ms B's house to do the latter's chores and get paid $2,000 per month for doing the work. At the same time Ms B, now with free time, goes to Ms A's house and do what Ms A would have done had she stayed home; Ms B gets paid $2,000 for this work. Although the total earnings of the two ladies fully offset each other, GDP is raised by $4,000 per month. Of course, they both will have to report their incomes to authorities and pay taxes and each is worse off because of the taxes. Any economic activity that does not go through the market is not included in the GDP figures. Therefore, the underground economy is excluded from the GDP figures as are *illegal* activities. However, economists have been hard at work trying to estimate non-market activities, with some success. Once estimated, these activities are included in the GDP; one such item is the *imputed* value of the rent for living in your own home (owner-occupied rent).

GDP includes only what is <u>produced</u> during the measurement period. This means that the value of houses already in place is not included. Nor is the price of used cars that are sold and bought. However, if you sell your car to a dealer for $1,800 and the dealer resells it for $2,200, the extra $400 is included in the GDP because an additional $400 worth of value has been created, whether or not the $400 was due to repairs made to the car or simply because the dealer found a customer for the car; just finding the right buyer creates value.

Measured GDP can grow as a result of a growing population, rising prices (i.e., inflation), increased productivity, and as more of what is produced goes through the market. If each person in the economy can produce $50,000 worth of products and services (collectively, we call them *goods*), then a larger number of people will produce more GDP; this is one reason that when we want to compare the well-being of people of different countries we us GDP per capita. Inflation also affects the size of the GDP; if peanuts cost $1.20 per pound in one year and $1.50 the next, and all other goods in the economy experience a rise in their prices, then the GDP will be higher in the second year even if the quantity of peanuts and other goods have not changed. To correct for the bias inflation creates, economists adjust for inflation to come up with what is called *real GDP*. Productivity is key; if each of us can produce more, then GDP increases. It is productivity that helps the per capita GDP to increase in the real sense; it is through productivity improvement that real GDP rises. If a larger portion of the underground economy (where the work and payment for that work is not reported to authorities) becomes public, then measured GDP rises as well. For the U.S., the underground economy is relatively insignificant.

The Size of the US Economy

As of the second quarter of 2018, the U.S. GDP was about $20.4 trillion, on an annual basis. That is, if the U.S. kept producing at the same rate as it was during April-June, 2018 through April-June, 2019 some $20.4 trillion worth of goods would be produced. To get a better idea of how well the economy is doing over time, economists use constant prices. They take one specific year's prices as "base" and measure other years' GDP using the base year prices. Currently the base year is 2012 and using that year, the current GDP is $18.5 trillion. The difference between $20.4 trillion and $18.5 trillion is due to rise in prices, not to more goods produced. It is useful to see what happened in terms of real GDP between the base year 2012 and now (2018 second quarter). In 2012, real GDP amounted to $16.2 trillion versus $18.5 trillion now, a 14.2% rise over the six years, or about 2.2% per annum. In other words, about 2% per year of the increase in nominal GDP was due to the rise in prices (inflation) during the past six years.

The value of each unit of good reflects incomes earned by suppliers of everything that goes into producing that good. The GDP can therefore be measured by the incomes received by workers and payments made to suppliers of material, rents paid, and so on.

To gain more perspective on the U.S. economy, we can compare various countries with the GDP of the U.S. The table below provides a picture. All the data are shown in US dollars. But there are two units of measurement: US dollars and PPP. PPP stands for *purchasing power parity*. Prices can be vastly different in different countries, especially for products that are not traded internationally. A haircut in China costs a lot less than the same haircut in the U.S. The prices of most foods and services are quite different across national borders. Therefore, without considering such cost of living variances one is presented with an inaccurate view of living standards. To adjust for such differences, PPP is used. Economists come up with estimates of prices in each region and make adjustments to dollar-measured GDPs.

Comparison of Gross Domestic Products, 2018

	GDP (trillion $)	GDP (trillion $), PPP
U.S.	20.4	20.4
China	12.2	23.2
European Union (EU)	12.6	20.9
Japan	5.0	5.6
Mexico	1.2	2.8
Canada	1.7	1.8

As shown in the above table, the US GDP in PPP terms is a shade lower than the EU's but some 12% lower than China's. On the other hand, the population of US stands at 327 million, as compared to China's 1,415 million, the EU's 510 million and Japans 127 million. On per capita terms, the US produces about $62,400 worth of GDP, versus $16,400 for China,

$41,000 for the EU, and $43,000 for Japan. After we adjust for cost of living differences, the average American produced nearly 4 times more GDP than a Chinese, and about 1.5 times more than a citizen of the EU or Japan.

GDP Composition

The GDP is the consequence of various types of economic activities. It is useful to classify to separate these activities into different groups, called *sectors*. It is the sum of the values of these sectors that determines the size of the GDP. The GDP is determined (or composed) according to:

GDP = Consumption + Investment + Government + Exports - Imports

Consumption amounts to about 2/3 of the total. It measures everything people spend on consumption goods: food, health care, education, insurance, housing, and so on. Investment is what businesses, governments, and consumers spend on factories, roads, housing, and similar items that enhance the capacity of the nation to produce. Government includes federal and state and local spending. Exports are products and services that are sold to foreigners, and include such things as equipment, design of high-tech equipment (e.g., iPhones), American consultants working for foreign businesses, American pilots flying foreign-owned airliners, and educating foreign students at U.S. universities.

Imports consist of stuff that American buy from other countries, such as TV sets made in Korea or China, cars made in Germany, and American tourists visiting foreign lands. Imports deduct from the domestic GDP because they are produced abroad; however, those who in the U.S. are employed in the imports business, such as truckers and retailers that move and sell the imported goods, contribute to the domestic GDP. When you buy a Chinese TV sets from your local department store, the salary of the salesperson who helped you is part of the domestic GDP.

Not everything that is produced is available to be consumed. Taxes must be paid. Some of the GDP is used to replenish used up (depreciated) equipment and to repair factories. After all such deductions and savings are taken into account, we come up with consumption expenditures of $13.9 trillion in 2018 (second quarter, at annual rate), of which $9.5 trillion was spent on services. Service include health care, vacations, haircuts, internet service, rent, education and so on. We spent relatively little on products such as cars, electronics, food, etc. Corporate profits amounted to $2.2 trillion.

Economy's Sectors

To get a better idea of the shape of the US economy, let us look at some sectors. Of a GDP of about $20 trillion, only $170 billion is contributed by agriculture and forestry, not even 1% of the total. About 11.7% is contributed by manufacturing. Finance and insurance amount to about 7.5%. All services combined contribute 48% of the total GDP; services play a far more important role in our economy than manufacturing.

The US exports about $2.6 trillion and imports some $3.3 trillion worth of products and services. Much of the US exports are in the form of services but imports very little in services. The trade deficit is thus around $550 billion. How do we pay for the deficit? Just like any private person, the shortage must be covered somehow: through borrowing or sale of assets. The US borrows by selling bonds to foreigners and sell assets by selling them houses, stocks in companies or businesses outright.

But the US has something few countries have: the US dollar is an international reserve currency. Many central banks all over the world hold US dollars. Let's say you import glassware worth $35,000 from Poland and you give the foreign seller $35,000 in US dollars. The seller cannot use dollars to buy grocery or clothes in her country. She may deposit it in a bank and receive some Zlotys and keep the rest in dollars. It turns out that the Polish bank is happy enough to hold onto those dollars. That kind of transactions take place all the time, with huge sums of US dollars held by foreigners; in many countries, the US dollars is often used for transactions in those countries and as hedge against inflation and lack of confidence in government policy. It is difficult to determine how many US dollars are kept abroad. A study done by the Federal Reserve some years ago estimated that in 1995 more than one-half of American dollars were kept abroad; there is no reason to think that things have changed since that study was done. It turns out that the vast majority of $100 bills are held by foreigners. So, the US can import cars and TV sets and in exchange give the foreign sellers pieces of paper with photos of our presidents and pictures of our monuments.

For investors one aspect of business sectors is quite important: How does a particular sector perform when the economy rises and falls (during the *business cycle*)? Some sectors are relatively immune to the ups and downs of the economy and some are quite sensitive to these cycles. Among the former are primary education, health care, utilities and food sectors. Among the latter are housing construction, travel, high-technology, business equipment and automobile manufacturing sectors. The stocks of sectors whose fortunes are relatively insensitive to business cycles are referred to as "defensive" stocks. The returns on defensive stocks tend to be less volatile but at the same time lower on average than other stocks.

Business Cycles: Growth, Recessions and Recoveries

The American economy grew by an average of around 4.1% during the decade of the 1960s, by just over 3% during the decade of the 1970s and close to 3.5% during the 1981-2000 period (all figures are adjusted for inflation). The economy grew by 2.8% per year during the entire 1948-2017 span. Unfortunately, the growth rate dropped to a slow 1.7% per year in the decade of 2000-2010, that included the Great

Recession of 2007-2009 (actual period: 2007 quarter 4 through 2009 quarter 2), followed by a growth of 2.1% per year during 2010-2017.

But the growth rates offered above are averages, covering periods of high as well as low rates, including period of negative growth rates, when the economy actually declined. When the economy declines, businesses lose money, people lose jobs, and incomes fall. Unemployment rises and opportunities disappear (unemployment rose to around 10% during the Great Recession of 2008; normally, it stands at an average of around 5%).

It is a characteristic of the U.S. economy to go through periods of expansion and contraction; the contractions or recessions occur about once every 6-8 years, although some expansions have lasted 8-10 years (see the diagram below); the current expansion is its tenth year as of October 2018. These contractions and expansions are referred to as business cycles. Various explanations have been offered by economists for the reasons the economy falls into a recession. The 2008 recession was apparently caused by a serious failure of the financial system as a result of widespread bankruptcies in the housing mortgages. The problem was that many homeowners carried adjustable mortgages on their homes and the Federal Reserve raised interest rates to combat inflation. As interest rates increased so did the mortgage rates of homeowners; these homeowners could no longer afford their mortgage payments and started selling their homes. Home prices, which had gone through the roof in the prior 4-5 years, collapsed, putting further pressure on sellers of houses; their equity had fallen to nil or even became negative. It was less onerous for these people to just walk away from their property than pay their mortgage.

U.S. Real GDP, 1947-2017

Source: *The Federal Reserve Bank of St. Louis. The vertical shaded areas represent recession periods.*

Holders of these mortgages, which included major mortgage and investment banks suffered massive losses. This, in turn, put pressure on issuers of mortgage insurance – such as the firm AIG, and the government-sponsored Freddie Mac and Fannie Mae; because of their role in the financial system and the economy, the latter three had to be rescued by the government, at the cost of tens of billions of dollars. These and some other financial institutions are now labelled by the government as "too big to fail" and essentially the government guarantees their survival; major banks such as J.P. Morgan, Wells Fargo, Bank of America are also among these "too big to fail" entities. Of course, this guarantee comes at the cost of closer control of these institutions by the government. However, the question remains why allow them to become so big in the first place and now that they are this big, why not break them up? Some have argued that there are economies of scale (i.e., the larger the business the lower its costs) and economies of scope (i.e., the more products and services produced by the business the lower its costs) of letting them increase in size; the lower costs are passed on to consumers. Others have argued that we must allow these entities grow larger because they have to compute on the world scene with foreign financial institutions as large or larger than the American financial firms.

Recessions in the United States are mostly shallow and brief, on average lasting about one year. In response, the Federal Reserve (the monetary authority in the U.S.) cuts interest rates to stimulate car buying and home purchases, and business investment. Fiscal policy, in the form of lower taxes and higher government spending (infrastructure expenditures, unemployment compensation, etc.) help maintain incomes and household wealth to keep expenditures from falling too sharply. To illustrate what takes place in a recession consider the anomalous Great Recession of 2008-2010. Home prices fell sharply and this wiped out $6 trillion in household wealth; by itself, this decline in household wealth reduced consumer spending by around $600 billion, amounting to about 1.5% in each of the three years 2008-2010.

An investor in stocks is interested in identifying which sectors are procyclical and which are not; those sectors whose performance is not highly correlated with business cycles provide a degree of protection against the economy's fluctuations and their stocks in those sectors which, as discussed above, are referred to as "defensive". In addition, an investor wants to know which *phase* of the business cycle we find ourselves in. If, for example, the economy has reached its trough and is on an upswing, the investor would switch out of defensive stocks and move her funds into procyclical stocks, such as housing and travel.

Inflation

There is often confusion about inflation and high prices. Inflation refers to rising prices, whether prices are low or high. You can have high inflation and low prices and low inflation and high prices. If an American travels to Japan or Switzerland, she will find prices quite high in those countries but these prices have remained fairly constant for several years; consequently, inflation is almost nonexistent in these two countries, and prices actually declined in Japan for some period, with *deflation* experienced there. On the other hand, Turkey's inflation amounted to around 10% in 2017 and does not seem to have abated by much since then, yet prices in Turkey are quite low.

Several years ago, the weekly "The Economist" started publishing the price of the Big Mac hamburgers in different countries. The focus was to see whether a country's foreign exchange rate was under- or overvalued. The rationale of using the Big Mac is that this item is almost identical everywhere, it requires similar inputs of meat, wheat (the bun), energy (for cooking and lighting), land (for the store and to produce the meat and wheat)), and labor (workers in the store and on the farm). While admittedly a crude measure, this idea has now become quite popular as a criterion to compare living costs in different regions. The price of a Big Mac is around $6.70 (with no inflation) in Switzerland, around $5.50 in the U.S. (with inflation of 2%) and $2.30 in Turkey (with inflation exceeding 7-8%).

As discussed above, inflation is a measure of changing prices, not the level of prices. We have various prices: at the consumer level; at the wholesale level; at the manufacturing level; price of goods we import or export; and for the economy as a whole, which includes import prices and export prices. Even at the consumer level we have different measures: urban consumers (CPI-U) versus urban wage earners and clerical workers (CPI-W). The Federal Reserve (the *Fed*) prefers the price measure for Personal Consumption Expenditures (PCE) since it covers a wider range of items. By any of these measures, inflation is quite low in the U.S. these days, running at around 2% per year. Inflation was quite high in the 1970s, reaching 11.3% in 1979, rising to 13.5% in 1980 and falling a little to 10.3%. The Federal Reserve raised interest rates drastically, choking off economic activity so that inflation fell to 3.2% by 1983; US inflation has amounted to around 3.1-3.2% for decades. As an investor, you want to keep an eye on what the Fed is up to.

Inflation influences investment and investors. As inflation increases, the Federal Reserve tends to raise the interest rates. With higher interest rates, economic activity slows down: businesses invest less in equipment and plants, people buy fewer cars and homes, and so on. Slower economic activity lowers company profits. In addition, the *cost of capital* that investors use to value stock rises. Both these effects cause stock prices to decline. As will be discussed in a later chapter, higher interest rates put downward pressure on bond prices, thus making bonds less attractive as well.

Chapter 2

THE FINANCIAL SYSTEM

A modern economy cannot function without a financial system. The U.S. has by far the most sophisticated and complex financial system in the world. Just imagine if there were no banks; without bank there would be no checking or savings accounts, and there would be no checks. You would be paid in cash, and you would have to carry cash with you all the time and save your money under the mattress or in a cookie jar. The invention of credit cards has made checks nearly superfluous. These are the most basic features of the financial system.

The Financial System's Features

The financial system currently goes far beyond these "primitive" attributes. It consists of a large variety of institutions, markets, and instruments. The financial system has evolved into what it is today because, despite its occasional failures, it provides a service to the economy in an efficient way. And the system is evolving continuously because new features render the system more useful and more efficient.

The financial system's main function is to bring people who buy and sell products and services together, help bring together those who have excess funds with those who are short of funds. As a corollary, the system also makes it possible for individuals to save for later when they would like to access their savings. The players in the system are *financial intermediaries* (also referred to as *financial institutions*) and their activities take place in *financial markets*. It is these markets through which funds flow.

Financial markets recycle the funds in the economy. Their function is to allocate the savings of individuals to various businesses and governments in need of funds. Some state and municipal governments (collectively referred to as municipal governments) are also net lenders, as they run budget surpluses. In other words, businesses are net borrowers of funds and individuals and some municipal governments are net lenders of funds. Businesses borrow to fund their activities, including starting new ventures or expansion of their enterprise. The US federal government has been a net borrower of funds in decades, with a few exceptions in some years. The federal borrowing is a consequence of its (tax) revenues falling short of its spending; this is the federal budget *deficit*. It is true that individuals also borrow to purchase assets, particularly houses and cars; but their borrowing is made possible by the savings of other individuals. Companies do some saving as well by not paying out as dividends all their profits, retaining such earnings. But overall, businesses are net borrower of funds.

A *market* is a physical location or a communication system where transactions take place. *Institutions* exist to facilitate these transactions using various instruments. For convenience and clarity these markets are classified.

An important component of the financial system is the *investment companies* which receive funds from the public and invests those funds for them. Because of their importance and diversity of their functions, organizations and objectives, a separate chapter covers them.

Primary Markets

These are markets in which users of funds raise money by issuing new securities. Users of funds are for the most part corporations but governments as well. They issue various financial instruments, basically stocks and bonds, to acquire the needed funds. New issues amounted to nearly $2.4 trillion in 2007, the year before the Big Recession. The new issues were $1.8 trillion by corporations and $0.4 trillion by local and state governments in 2017.

Initial public offerings (IPOs) issue securities in primary markets as well. These are securities that new ventures going public for the first time sell to investors. The regulations permitting initial offerings are different, and more restrictive, than regulations on trading already-issued securities which are traded in secondary markets.

Secondary Markets

Once financial instruments have been issued they trade in secondary markets. The original issuer of these securities does not obtain funds when these instruments are traded. Secondary markets play a critical function, however. They provide information to investors and the issuing company the market's valuation of the business – for example, are the company's activities enhancing the shareholders' value? And the secondary markets make it easy for investors to buy and sell shares of the company: they provide liquidity.

Money Markets and Capital Markets

The financial markets are also classified along the maturity dimension of the securities. In reality there is no difference between money markets and capital markets; the distinction is artificial. Securities maturing in one year or less are said to be traded in money markets. Any security with maturity longer than one year is said to be traded in capital markets.

The U.S. Treasury Department

As in any sizeable business, the government needs a treasury. In the United States, one of the important departments is the U.S. Treasury Department, headed by a cabinet member. The Treasury Department is responsible for raising revenue and disbursing funds in behalf of the

Federal government. It collects taxes – the Internal Revenue Service (IRS) is part of the Treasury – and sells government bonds and make payments to meet the government's obligations. It is also responsible for the exchange rate between the U.S. dollar and other currencies.

The U.S. Treasury Building in Washington, D.C., with the statue of Alexander Hamilton, the first Secretary of the Treasury (1789-1795)

Alongside the U.S. Treasury, at the top of the financial system stands a central bank. The central bank in the U.S. is the *Federal Reserve System* (the "Fed"). The Fed plays a critical role in the U.S. economy.

The Federal Reserve

Why do interest rates change? As discussed later there are a host of interest rates, some for loans lasting a few hours, some lasting for decades. The Canadian Pacific Corporation has issued bonds that do not mature for 1,000 years (yes, one thousand years). More down-to-earth maturities are the one hundred-year bonds issued by Disney and Coca-Cola. In the U.K. you have bonds that <u>never</u> mature, called *consols*; these just pay interest but you can never collect the face value (principal); however, you can convert them to cash by selling them to another investor. At the other extreme are funds that banks often borrow from each other for a few hours (overnight), to cover some legal requirements, called *reserves*.

Interest is the price for the "use" of money. In general, when there is a great demand for funds and few willing lenders, just like the price of apples and peanuts, the interest rate rises.

A modern economy has a central bank that has the authority to print money and conduct monetary policy. In the U.S. this central bank is called the Federal Reserve Bank, seated in Washington, D.C., and it is popularly known as *the Fed*. Like pretty much everything else in America, we prefer a decentralized system. Accordingly, the Federal Reserve System consists of 12 Federal Reserve Banks, one in each of the 12 Federal Reserve Districts. As you might expect, most of these Banks are located in the East. However, one of the largest Districts is the San Francisco Bank that covers Alaska, Hawaii, Washington, Oregon, California, Arizona, Nevada, Utah, Idaho, the American Samoa, Guam, and Northern Mariana Islands. Then there is the Kansas City Bank and St. Louis Bank – just "minutes", about 250 miles apart – both in Missouri! The reason for that arrangement is that when the legislation was being considered to establish the Fed, a very powerful legislator insisted on this setup – some say for no good reason, just pure and plain politics. Recently, some researcher at (guess where) the St Louis Fed has come up with an argument that the Missouri region was significant enough to justify two Fed Banks in that neighborhood! If it was justified to have two Fed banks in Missouri then we should have a dozen of Fed banks between Boston, MA and Richmond, VA.

At the center of the Fed is a seven-member Board of Governors. The Board supervises District banks, which are the operating arm of the system. An important committee of the system is the *Federal Open Market Committee* (FOMC), consisting of the seven members of the Board, the president of the New York Fed bank, and four presidents of the remaining district banks on a rotating basis. The FOMC sets monetary policy: the quantity of money and interest rates.

Location and Areas of District Federal Reserve Banks

Source: *Federal Reserve Bulletin*, Board of Governors of the Federal Reserve System.

The Fed is a non-profit, government entity; it is independent of the executive and legislative branches. It holds massive amounts of Treasury securities which it uses as an instrument of monetary policy; in recent years the Fed has acquired private sector bonds as well. The interest it earns on these securities is used to finance its operations; what is left is returned to the U.S. Treasury.

The Fed has a significant impact on the stock market. To illustrate, the stock market had entered a period of weakness after the Fed had announced that it would push interest rates up over the next year or two; the market had declined by 3.8% between November 16, 2018 and November 23, 2018. On November 28, 2018, in a speech the Fed Chairman pronounced that the current fed fund rate (the interest rate most closely controlled by the Fed) was "just" below its normal level. The markets took this to mean that the Fed would not raise rates by much. As a result, the market shot up over the next few days, by nearly 3%.

Commercial Banks

Commercial banks are financial institutions that are allowed to accept deposits from clients, hence they are referred to as *depository institutions*. Checking and savings accounts are created when a client deposits cash in the bank. The bank, in turn, lends money to individuals and businesses. Individuals borrow money to buy houses ("mortgages"), automobiles, furniture and appliances, and so forth. Businesses borrow to run their operations, buy equipment, etc. Commercial banks are the largest group by asset size among depository institutions. As recently as the mid-1980s there were over 14,000 commercial banks in the U.S. Their number has shrunk down to around 4,800 currently. The main service provided by commercial banks, in their strictly banking activities, is lending. They take short-term deposits and lend longer term. Most of the time, short term interest rates are lower than longer term interest rates and it is the gap between what banks pay to depositors (the short term rates) and what they earn on their loans (the long term rates) that is the source of much of their profit.

Banks must contend with *adverse selection* and *moral hazard*. Adverse selection is the situation that those who can least afford it are the ones most eager to borrow. Moral hazard arises when once an individual obtains a loan, he may not use the borrowed funds for the designated purpose (e.g., a person may get a loan to build a house but uses the money for a nice vacation in the Bahamas; to prevent this from happening, the bank disperses the funds gradually as the building progresses) or be less vigilant in expending them. Both adverse selection and moral hazard arise in insurance as well, but in a different context.

Commercial banks are highly regulated. They are supervised by the Fed, as well as a host of other federal and state agencies. National banks are those that are chartered and regulated by the Office of the Comptroller of the Currency; these are among the largest banks in the U.S. and they are <u>required</u> to become members of the Federal Reserve System. The Federal Deposit Insurance Corporation (FDIC) insures deposits, up to a $250,000 currently, and is also involved in banking regulation. Commercial banks are the primary route through which the Fed's monetary policy is implemented. The Fed achieves its policy goals mainly by injecting money into and withdrawing money from commercial banks.

A *run* on a bank occurs when a large number of depositors withdraw or attempt to withdraw their funds. The cause for a run is the news, fake or real, that the bank is going bankrupt or running out of cash. What compels depositors to withdraw their deposits is the "first-come, first-serve" procedure banks follow: people at the top of the line get to take their money out until the bank runs out of cash. Those in the back of the line end up losing their deposits. Therefore, the incentive is to "run" to the bank and withdraw your money as soon as possible. Of course, such runs can happen to any depository institution. The insurance the FDIC provides eliminates this incentive.

Savings Institutions

Savings institutions too accept deposits. They convert short term deposits to long term loans and the gap between interest rates paid on short term borrowing and long term loans provides these institutions with profits. Their origin goes back to the early 1800s. In those days, they pooled savings and invested in mortgages for the most part. This is their most important service to this day, although they also provide many of the functions of the commercial banks these days. Savings institutions invested heavily in real estate in the 1980s; when real estate prices collapsed there was a crisis in this sector. Many of them (more than 1,200), mostly organized as Savings and Loans (S&L) went bankrupt and had to be rescued by the government, at tax payer expense of course. The Office of Thrift Supervision is the main regulator of savings institutions. Similar to commercial banks, the FDIC insures deposits at these institutions, up to $250,000 per account.

Credit Unions

Credit unions (CU) are depository institutions but are nonprofit *mutual* organizations, owned by their members; a depositor of a CU becomes a member. To organize a CU, members must have something in common, such as occupation (e.g., firemen CU), covering a specific community, or an association. Each CU determines the common bond of its members, as long as the CU regulator approves. The size of a member's deposit determines that member's share in the CU. The deposits are lent to members; members use loans to fund mortgages on their homes, to buy cars, and for other needs. These loans are the main source of the CU's earnings which are paid out as interest to depositors. CUs invest in other securities, such as US Treasurys, as well.

Since CUs are nonprofit entities, they are tax-exempt. This means that their loans can and do carry lower interest rates than loans from other lenders while they can pay higher rates to depositors. Banks claim that the tax breaks given to CUs constitute an unfair competitive advantage.

CUs can be chartered by states or the federal government. The federally chartered CUs, numbering around 7,000, are regulated by the National Credit Union Administration. Each account is insured up to $250,000.

Finance Companies

Finance companies are in the business of making loans. They do not accept deposits; instead they fund their lending from money invested by shareholders and from borrowing from other sources, such as banks.

They are quite specialized in that some lend to consumers (e.g., Household Finance), some to businesses (e.g., U.S. Bancorp Equipment Finance and CIT Group), and others are "captive" since they finance the purchases made from specific companies (e.g., Honda Financial Services). One important function of "business" finance companies is factoring: they buy the account receivable from companies at a discount to their face value and they take the responsibility of collecting them.

Insurance Companies

Insurance involves the payment by an insurance company to the insured if a prespecified adverse event occurs. In exchange, the insured pays premiums to the insurance company. Insurance companies earn their income from premiums policyholders pay and from returns on the investment they make. The insurance companies' investments are funded by the premiums. Insurance companies are chartered and supervised by states. Insurance services cover two major categories: (1) life and health, and (2) property and casualty. Property and casualty provides protection against personal injury and liability due to accidents, fire, and theft. *Credit default swaps* (CDS) is a form of insurance that is relatively new. CDS covers the loan in the event that the borrower defaults; like ordinary insurance, the insured makes regular premium payments to the insurance company that has issued the CDS. These premiums rose immensely during the 2008 financial crisis.

When it comes to life insurance, there is large number of alternative kinds of policy. Only three types of policy are mentioned here. *Term life* has a maturity after which time it is no longer in effect; beneficiary receives the value of the contract if death occurs prior to the maturity of the contract. *Whole life* has no expiration and the policyholder can borrow against the cash value of the contract. *Universal life* has no expiration and the premiums are invested in mutual funds; if the returns are low (e.g., if interest rates are low or the stock market falls), then premiums can rise, making the payment of premiums onerous for retired policyholders. Many life insurance policies are a blend of "insurance" and "investment or savings". It is best to separate the insurance component from the investment and savings components.

A major issue that insurance companies face is, similar to lending institutions, moral hazard and adverse selection. For insurance companies, moral hazard refers to the situation that the policyholder's behavior can change because of insurance: the insured tends to become less risk averse. For example, the homeowner, once she has fire insurance, becomes less careful in avoiding activities that can cause a fire; or, a driver who has adequate insurance my become a reckless driver. Adverse selection is when the riskiest individuals purchase insurance; thus, the more serious is a person's health outlook, the more likely is he to buy health insurance. This is one of the problems that the Affordable Care Act has confronted since the younger, healthier individuals have chosen to not participate in the national system; this has led to higher insurance premiums for the rest who tend to be older.

Securities Firms and Investment Banks

These financial institutions serve as brokers transferring funds from net suppliers of funds (e.g., consumers) to net users of funds (e.g., businesses). Investment banks help various organizations sell securities. These banks play a critical role in taking new companies public through initial public offerings (IPO). Their activities include advising businesses on restructuring and on mergers and acquisitions (M&A). When the founders of a new business want to grow the business but lack the funds to support the growing business, they need to go outside to raise the money. They may be able to borrow, but lenders can impose strict rules on what the company can or cannot do, and these rules may constrain the growth of the business; also, since interest payments are fixed, these payments may become onerous on a small and growing business.

Alternatively, they can sell shares to outsiders. One way to raise funds from outsiders is to sell shares to the public at large. When a business sells shares to the public for the first time it is referred to as *initial public offering*. They also help entities, public and private, to sell securities. To become a public company the business has to comply with lots of rules, both federal and state. Investment banks play a critical role in assisting businesses becoming public companies. The main federal agency responsible for ensuring that public companies meet the various regulations is the Securities and Exchange Commission, the SEC.

Securities firms are engaged in secondary market for securities, that is, existing securities that were issued in the past and are now being sold and bought by investors. Some of the larger financial institutions are engaged in both investment banking and brokering securities.

Check Cashing Businesses and Loan Sharks

According to the government, about 7% of households did not have a bank account in 2015. Another 20% had a savings or checking account but obtained financial services from outside of the banking system. There are about 126-million households in the U.S. so nearly 9-million households are outside of the banking system altogether and 25-million rely on the nonbank system for some of their financial service needs.

Check cashing businesses cover some of these services. The general practice is to cash a person's check at a discount to the nominal value of the check. The discount covers the risk of the check bouncing as well as the opportunity cost of not earning interest on the funds. If the check is being cashed in a retail store – usually, a neighborhood grocery store – the store also requires the client to make purchases. The interest rate charged on the service tends to be quite high. In some states there are *usury* laws which specify a ceiling on the interest a lender may charge a borrower.

Loan sharks are individuals who lend money for a very short period at very high rates of interest. The lender may resort to violence against the borrower for nonpayment (e.g., broken knees!).

Both loan sharks and check cashing services fulfill an unmet need.

Chapter 3

FINANCIAL MARKETS: EFFICENT OR INEFFICENT?

In the mid-1960s economists (Paul Samuelson and Eugene Fama) hit on the idea that financial markets are *efficient*. Efficient means that any and all information about a security is instantaneously impounded in its price. The reason this happens is because of intense competition in the securities market by well-informed, rational investors, and these investors work hard to earn as much money as possible. Any news about the security is analyzed by the market and the market acts on the available information which, in turn, determines the security price. All of that occurs quite fast, and the security prices adjust so that securities are neither underpriced nor overpriced. This means that one shouldn't waste one's time trying to determine the price of a security; the market does it for us. Among the implications of this hypothesis that financial markets are efficient is that randomly selecting securities to invest in is just as good as any other strategy.

In recent decades economists (or at least some of them) have questioned the validity of this hypothesis. For example, why would anyone spend the time and the money to study the impact of any news on the price of a security if its price accurately reflects everything there is to know about that security? And if nobody does, how does the price of a security adjust to new information? In addition, it is glaringly true that mispricing is quite widespread and security prices move slowly and gradually in response to new information. For instance, there is ample evidence that when the takeover of one company by another is announced, prices of the stocks of both companies adjust to their new prices gradually over several days, whereas the efficient market hypothesis requires that the full price adjustment happens immediately (usually, the stock of the acquiring company experiences a decline while the target company's stock rises in prices). And numerous studies by psychologists and neurologists have conclusively demonstrated that individuals, when it comes to investing, are not anything close to computing machines seeking maximum earnings in a mathematical way. For example, we regret losing money more than we enjoy earning it.

As an alternative to the *efficient market hypothesis* (EMH) is *behavioral economics* (BE). BE accepts that individuals are not automatons in their economic decisions and, often enough, we make poor investments, and when faced with alternatives, frequently we choose irrationally. When it comes to investing, conventional economics focusses on risk and return. BE admits that how an individual "feels" about the company under consideration influences her investment decision; e.g., some individuals avoid investing in companies in the tobacco, oil, or defense industries, even if these firms offered superior risk-adjusted investment opportunities. More recently, Andrew Lo, drawing on the work of evolutionary scientists, psychologists and neurologists has proposed that markets continually evolve and, in response, investors change their behavior to increase their earnings. As "evolution" implies, the process is sluggish and gradual.

If the EMH is imperfect, then security prices can be mispriced. And if there is mispricing, there is room for earning returns that are market-beating – that is, higher than the risk-adjusted level. Therefore, a *passive* approach to investing is suboptimal. Passive investing means selecting stocks at random or simply buying the entire market, without changing one's portfolio. However, as discussed later, selecting the stocks that provide the highest risk-adjusted returns requires an extreme level of forecasting ability which most investors do not possess.

If many investors are less-than-perfectly rational, an individual who acts strictly for pure economic gains can achieve an advantage and earn above market returns. But keep in mind that one can be correct in her assessment of the situation yet lose money if she acts on that evaluation; this can occur if the market behaves sub-optimally and moves against the lone investor who acts optimally. For example, you may correctly forecast that a stock will rise and buy it; however, the market may cause the stock to fall for an extended period due to the market's faulty assessment; you may run out of money by the time the market corrects its assessment.

Daniel Kahneman tells the story of analyzing the performance, based on their stock picking, of wealth managers of a financial advisory firm. The 25 managers' year-end bonusses depended on their performance ranking. After looking at how consistent these managers had been picking stocks over eight years, he concluded that he could not detect skill among them – their performance was random. And since their compensation was based on their ranking, the firm was rewarding them for luck. It seems that throwing dice to select stock is just as good.

Other researchers have found that individuals lose consistently in their stock selection: dice rolling monkeys outperform this outcome. Individuals sell winning stocks and they buy losing stocks. Even among professional fund managers, 2/3 of them underperform the market in any given year. Furthermore, in year-to-year performance of funds, the correlation is nearly zero, meaning that funds that outperformed the market had a good roll of the dice in that particular year. It is also observed that investors react asymmetrically to stock gains and losses: losses hurt much more than gains feel good.

Dice-rolling monkeys outperform investors

Chapter 4

PRESENT VALUE, FUTURE VALUE

There is a difference between $1 today versus the same $1 in ten years. This difference arises from the observation that people prefer receiving $1 now rather than wait some time to receive $1 in the future; people are impatient and discount the value of money that they acquire in the future. They apply a discount rate to future cash flow. This is referred to as *time preference*. In other words, $1 received at different times can be more or less valuable (to the recipient). To compare $1 received at different times, we bring their values to the present.

The past is past (sunk cost), and the present is more valuable than the future

One-Period Cash Flow

How do we measure the difference in the value of $1 received today versus $1 received in the future? An obvious way to do this measurement is to ask the individual "how much are you willing to take in <u>one year</u> if you give up $1 <u>today</u>?" Suppose she answers $1.080. The value $1.080 that she provides is called *future value* (FV) of $1. What amounts to the same thing is to ask that person "how much are you willing to accept today for $1 that is coming to you in one year?" Let's say her answer is $0.926; we call $0.926 the *present value* (PV) of $1 to be received in one year. It is more intuitive to work with present values so most of the time the focus is on PV.

How did she come up with FV=1.080 and PV=0.926? To her, $1 today is worth 8% more than $1 one year from now. The 8% represents the *rate of interest* she wants to (or can) earn on her money. Therefore, she is indifferent between having $0.926 today or wait to receive $1.000 in one year. But what we <u>would like</u> to receive in the form of interest may be different from what we can receive because the rate of interest is determined by the market. To illustrate you may want to receive 6% on a savings account at your bank but if all the banks in your region offer 2.7% on such accounts, you too will have to settle for the same 2.7% – or not have a savings account at all.

Suppose you receive $100 today and the going (market) rate of interest is 6%; if you invest this money you end up with $106.00 in one year and $112.36 in two years. Thus, you would be equally happy to receive $100 today or $106 in one year – that is, the present value of $106 next year is $100. Similarly, the present value of $112.36 in two years is $100. Put another way, the future value of $100 in one year is $106.00 and the future value of $100 in two years is $112.36.

Now suppose that the rate of interest you can earn is 8% and you are offered the same $106.00 in one year. Which do you prefer, $100 now or $106.00 in one year? If you invest the $100 at 8%, you finish the year with $108.00 which is more than the $106.00 you have been offered; of course, you prefer the $100 you get today. In other words, the present value of $106.00 In one year is now worth less than $100. PV changes as the rate of interest changes. For those who are fond of algebra, the formula used to calculate present value ($106 at 6%) is

$$PV = \frac{\$106}{(1.06)} = \$100$$

And the present value of $106 at 8% is

$$PV = \frac{\$106}{1.08} = \$98.15$$

The 1.06 and 1.08 are obtained by adding "1" to the rates of interest of 6% and 8%, respectively, except that it is more common (and more correct in this context) to use the decimal version that divides the rate by 100, to get 0.06 and 0.08, respectively. Whichever version one uses, these rates are referred to as *discount rates* and the inverse of 1.06 or 1.08 (i.e., $\frac{1}{1.06} = 0.9434$ or $\frac{1}{1.08} = 0.9259$) are called *discount factors*.

Here is another way to look at present value. Suppose a financial institution tells you that you can earn an interest rate of 5% on your money and that if you don't touch your account (that is, if you leave your money in that account) for 3 years without taking any money out, not the principal and nor the interest earnings, you will have accumulated $120 by the end of the third year. How much do you have to deposit now to end up with $120 (which is the future value, FV)? The answer is the PV of $120 and it is obtained as $120/(1+.05)^3$ = $103.66. This is a very useful relationship. Let's say that you want to retire in 8 years and want to have $200,000 at that time; a financial institution tells you that they can invest your funds at 7% per year for 8 years. How much do you need to deposit with them to accumulate FV= $200K by the time you retire? The solution is to find the PV of this FV; the answer is $116,401.82 (=$200,000/1.07^8).

You may have noticed that as a cash flow is pushed farther and farther into the future, its PV becomes smaller and smaller. A cash flow has a lower PV the more distant it is. This is in part because people are "impatient" in the sense that they prefer receiving money and goods as close to the present as possible compared to having them in the more distant future.

To induce people to wait before receiving funds, they must be offered a little more money. Let's say you have won a $100 bet. I offer you three alternatives: receive the $100 right now, wait for 1 year, or wait for 2 years. I ask you to express your preference. Since you are likely similar to most homo sapiens you inform me that you rank the alternatives as follows: receive the money now, followed by receiving it in 1 year, and the least desirable alternative is to wait for 2 years. Why? Because waiting to receive money or goods is less gratifying than obtaining them immediately. That is one reason why so many Americans, perhaps up to one-half have no savings and so many spend beyond their means; they just can't postpone what they desire until they can better afford it. In our betting example, you state that you would be indifferent between receiving $100 now, $104 in 1 year, or $109 in 2 years. These extra dollars, the $4 and the $9, are compensation for you to wait, for 1 year or for 2 years, respectively.

The extra amounts also cover the possibility of my disappearing from the face of the earth, going bankrupt, or simply refusing to pay off my bet. In other words, postponing payments involves *risk*; the extra $4 and $9, which are interest payments, compensate you for your risk as well. And the longer the payment is postponed, the greater is the risk and, hence, the more you want to get paid; the longer is the maturity of a bond the riskier the bond is considered to be.

Multiperiod Uniform Cash Flows

You win lottery's big prize of $330 million. The big prize of $330 million is paid in equal annual increments over 30 years, $11 million per year. But the lottery administrators also give you the option of taking your prize in lump sum now. However, you are not given the full $330 million in lump sum; they give you the amount that if invested at some rate of return that can pay an annual amount (called *annuity*) that accrues to $330 million over the 30-year period. This is the present value (PV) of $11 million per year stretched over 30 years. This sort of multiperiod cash flow is quite common. A bond provides interest payments over several periods until the bond matures. A stock often pays quarterly dividends. A homeowner with a mortgage makes monthly payments to pay down the loan. How do we calculate the PV of such cash flows? We simply calculate the PV of each future cash flow and add them all up.

If offered $100 today versus different amounts in the future you decide that $104 a year hence or $109 two years hence are equivalent to $100 now – that is, you are indifferent between receiving $100 today or $104 in 1 year or $109 in 2 years. As mentioned above, economists prefer working with what they call *present value* (sometimes it is helpful to bring oneself down to the level of economists!). In your case, you calculated the PVs in your mind with the two future cash flows of $104 and $109. The way economists do this is to take the cash flows and divide them by the rate of interest: 4.000% per year for the one-year deal and 4.403% per year for the two-year deal; 4.403% becomes 9.000% when *compounded* for two years. Let's see how this compounding works.

If you have $1.00 and invest it at 4.403% per year for two years, you earn an interest of $0.04403 in the first year. In the second year, you earn $0.04403 on your original $1.00 but you also earn 4.403% on your interest earning of $0.04403; that amounts to $0.00194 for a total of $0.04403 + $0.00194 = $0.04597 in the second year. Add the two and you end up with

$$\$0.04403 + \$0.04597 = \$0.0900,$$

which is exactly 9% of $1.00. There is another way of looking at compounding. Your $1.00 becomes $1.04403 after one year and this $1.04403 earns an interest of 4.403% during the second year. We can also write $1.04403 in the form of [1 + 0.04403].

$$\$1.00 \longrightarrow [1 + 0.04403]$$

($1.00 becomes $1+$0.04403 after one year)

At the end of year 2 the term in the brackets earns interest of [1 + 0.04403] × 0.004403 but you also have the value that has accumulated in one year, namely, your [1 + 0.04403].

After two years you have [1 + 0.04403] from year one plus [1 + 0.04403] ×0.004403, or

$$[1 + 0.04403] + [1 + 0.04403] \times 0.004403.$$

Of course you remember how to take common factors, so this expression can be "simplified" to

$$[1 + 0.04403] \times [1 + 0.004403] = (1 + 0.004403)^2$$

Now, isn't this a beauty? Of course, it is. What if you had a 3-year loan at the same rate 4.403%? That's when using the last algebraic term becomes really useful. Instead of $(1 + 0.004403)^2$ with the exponent "2", we can use the exponent "3" as in $(1 + 0.004403)^3$. With a 4-year loan we use "4", and so on, for any number of years.

You have decided that you are willing to take $100 now or $104 in one year or $109 in two years. What you have decided is that the subjective value to you of $104 in one year is the same as $100 now, and $109 in two year is worth to you the same as $100 today. This boils down to saying that the *present value* of $104 is $100 and the *present value* of $109 is $100. You bring all future values to the present. In other words, you *discount* these future values to their present value equivalents. How do you that? You ask what is the rate of interest, or the rate of *discount*, that causes $100 grow to $104 or $109? Fortunately, there is a high school algebraic formula that does that for us. For the one-year 4.00% case,

$$\frac{1}{(1 + 0.0400)} \times \$104 = \$100$$

and for the two-year loan at 4.403%,

$$\frac{1}{(1 + 0.04403)^2} \times \$109 = \$100$$

Let us generalize a bit to make life simpler, but not less correct. This is done by assuming that all future discount rates remain the same as today. We do this because forecasting correctly what interest rates (or discount rates) will be in the distant future is very, very difficult; if you can forecast accurately then you will become extremely rich quickly. As long as we are using the same discount rate for all future cash flows we might as well use a "generic" rate and call it r. And let's use the generic notation t for the number of years a loan is taken. Then for any discount rate and any maturity, we can write

$$\frac{1}{(1+r)^t} \times F = P$$

Call this expression the *discounting formula*. This is general expression that can be used to calculate the present (or discounted) value, P, of any future value, F, for any maturity, t, and any discount (or interest) r. Sorry for using math, but it is nearly impossible not to use a bit of algebra to help us better understand securities. And since you have been so patient and interested, we might as well show what else one can do with this algebraic equation: given any current cash and interest rate and future time (say, your retirement time), you can calculate the future value of the current cash amount. All you have to do is to manipulate the discounting formula to obtain

$$F = P \times (1+r)^t.$$

Let's see if this works for the 2-year loan at 4.403% per year. The discount factor is

$$\frac{1}{(1+.04403)^2} = \frac{1}{1.09} = 0.91743;$$

when you multiply this value by $109, you get $100. So the present value of $109 is $100.

The neat thing about the discounting formula is that you can add up all future cash flows to determine the present value of their sum –here's the one for 4 years, $50 in each year, starting with the first payment one year from now.

$$\$173.25 = \frac{1}{(1+0.06)^1} \times 50 + \frac{1}{(1+0.06)^2} \times 50 + \frac{1}{(1+0.06)^3} \times 50 + \frac{1}{(1+0.06)^4} \times 50$$
$$= 47.17 + 44.50 + 41.98 + 39.60$$

First, note that the present value of the same $50 becomes progressively smaller as it is calculated for the more distant future; that is, distant-future cash flows are more heavily discounted than the near-future flows. Second, even though you get a total of $200 over the four-year period, the PV (or discounted value) of $200 is only $173.25.

Multiperiod Varying Cash Flows

The above discounting formula can be generalized to the case where cash flows vary from one period to the next. Here is an example with each future cash flow different: $F1$, $F2$, $F3$, and $F4$.

$$P = \frac{1}{(1+r)^1} \times F1 + \frac{1}{(1+r)^2} \times F2 + \frac{1}{(1+r)^3} \times F3 + \frac{1}{(1+r)^4} \times F4$$

= discounted value of $F1$ + discounted value of $F2$ + discounted value of $F3$ + discounted value of $F4$

Suppose that you win an unusual lottery that pays you $50 per year in each of the next 4 years, starting in one year. With the last payment you get an extra $1,000, for a total of $1050. Let's say that you can invest your funds at 6% per year (0.06 in decimal form); this 6% is the discount rate. What is the present value of these cash flows? Applying the above formula we get:

$$\$965.35 = \frac{1}{(1+0.06)^1} \times 50 + \frac{1}{(1+0.06)^2} \times 50 + \frac{1}{(1+0.06)^3} \times 50 + \frac{1}{(1+0.06)^4} \times 1050$$

$$= 47.17 + 44.50 + 41.98 + 831.70$$

There are many situations where the cash flows change from one period to another. For example, a stock's dividends can (and usually does) change from one period to the next. And there are bonds whose interest varies depending on all sorts of factors, such as the interest paid on Treasury bonds or foreign exchange rates. All that needs to be done to handle such cases is to change the value of the cash flows, from $50 in the above example to whatever the cash turns out to be. To illustrate, if the first year's payment is $35, the second year's is $58, followed by $72 in the third year, with final payment being $982, the new PV is

$$\$922.93 = \frac{1}{(1+0.06)^1} \times 35 + \frac{1}{(1+0.06)^2} \times 58 + \frac{1}{(1+0.06)^3} \times 72 + \frac{1}{(1+0.06)^4} \times 982$$

$$= 33.02 + 51.62 + 60.45 + 777.84$$

Now consider stocks. Since stocks pay cash in the form of dividends in future years, when interest rates rise, we need to calculate the present value of these cash flows to determine the value of stocks. That is how analysts put a value on stocks. They forecast all future cash flows (yes, all future cash flows, at times 10-15 years out and beyond), they then calculate the present value of these cash flows, sum these up and voilà, you have the current stock price.

As mentioned earlier, when the periodic payments stay the same, including the last one, this is called an annuity. For example, you invest with some institutions (such as an insurance company) for a number of years after which you receive a constant flow of cash for a definite period of time; a mortgage is an example of an annuity. If the payments continue for an indefinite period, it is called a *perpetuity* – a consol is a perpetuity. A growing annuity has the cash flows growing, as is the case for a growing perpetuity.

Chapter 5

INCOME AND WEALTH

People often refer to *income* and *wealth* as though they mean the same thing. And often we call some people rich. Who is rich, a 75-year old person who lives in a $2-million house in San Francisco relying on his social security of $1,500 and a pension of $1,200 a month, or a 27-year old computer whiz renting a $4,000 a month apartment in Boston making $180,000 a year but without any assets such as a house or stocks? The old man bought his house 50 years ago for around $18,000 and paid it off some 30 years ago; otherwise, he couldn't afford to buy it now. He could sell the house and move to Idaho and be able to afford a great deal more, but his kids and grand-children live in the Bay Area. They help him whenever he needs assistance and, besides, he doesn't feel he needs anything else. As you see, the label rich is vague.

That is why we have the two concepts: income and wealth. The old man is wealthy with little income. The young woman earns a high income but she is not wealthy

Income

Income has a time flow associated with it, such as a wage rate of $18 *per hour* or $350 *per week* or $43,000 *per year*. This is in contrast to having $18 in your wallet or $350 in your bank account. Income is a *flow* of funds that comes into your possession periodically. For most of us we *earn* some wage or salary over some time period; for this reason, sometimes income is referred to as earnings – the two terms are used interchangeably in this book.

What do you do with your income? Depending on how much you earn, you *spend* (in decades past, some called spending "outgo" – the opposite of "income") some of the income and you *save* some of it; what you save, for obvious reason, is called *savings*. A good chunk of your spending is on stuff that is used up pretty much in a very short time, such as on food or gasoline for your car, on postage, medicine or a visit to the doctor. These items bring immediate but short-lasting pleasure (e.g., food) or fulfill short-lasting needs (e.g., gasoline, medication). Economists call these items *consumption* goods. In general, anything that lasts one year or less is considered a consumption good. Some of what you spend goes to buy stuff that lasts a long time, such as a car, a computer, furniture, and similar items that fulfill needs or bring pleasure over a long period of time. Obviously these items (referred to as assets) are different from what we call consumption goods. We'll come back to this issue shortly.

What do you do with the money you do not spend, your savings? You can put it in a checking account, a saving account, under your mattress or in a cookie jar. There are lots of other things you can do with what you save. We'll devote much of this book to this issue. The objective is to help you make good decisions with these savings, to help you provide adequate funds in case of emergencies and enjoy a comfortable life now and when you retire.

Wealth

The money you do not spend is of course saved. Regardless of what you do with your savings, they accumulate into larger and larger sums. This is *wealth* as distinguished from income.

To better clarify the distinction, consider the bathtub and the faucet or valve that is pouring water into it; you can measure the flow of water but can also measure the amount of water that has been collected in the tub at any moment in time. When you are ready for a bath you turn the water on to fill the tub. At 3:47 p.m. the water is flowing at 2 gallons per minute and there is 16 gallons of water accumulated in the bathtub – the 2 gallons per minute of flow is like income, and the 16 gallons collected in the tub is like wealth. A minute later at 3:48 p.m. the bathtub contains 18 gallons of water which is analogous to saying that your (water) wealth has increased. A cow itself is *wealth* and the daily milk she gives is *income*.

For most people, wealth results from the accumulation of income not spent. Some lucky folks get some or all of their wealth from inheritance. Even luckier folks acquire their wealth from winning the lottery. It is true that some winners choose to receive their winnings over a number of years so this might be considered income rather than wealth; but what these lucky people have done is that they have decided to hand over their wealth to the lottery authorities and receive portions of it over a number of years.

When you save money out of your income, the accumulated wealth is in the form of money (also called *cash*) kept under your mattress or in a bank account. Your lottery winning too is in the form of money. But inherited wealth is most often in the form of real estate, stocks and bonds. Money, real estate, stocks and bonds, no matter how they are obtained, are referred to as *assets*. Your bank accounts, car, furniture, appliances, and home are assets as well, as are jewelry, baseball cards, and art work. Well, you too can accumulate your wealth in these other forms; i.e., you can use your cash asset to acquire other assets – you can convert your money asset to non-money assets. Indeed, you can convert any of your assets to other asset forms.

We can categorize assets into two broad groups: *financial* assets and *non-financial* assets. Financial assets include money, stocks and bonds and other securities. Non-financial assets include all other assets.

Most people convert most of their money asset to other assets. Why would you want to do that? Because money does not provide any pleasure directly – at least not for many people. Nor is money useful, other than making some transactions easy (or meeting emergencies that are require cash); actually, the usefulness of money for transactions is diminishing with new technologies such as credit cards, digital transactions, and so on. In contrast, many other assets provide pleasure and use. A car makes it possible for you to travel or to show off; your home makes it possible for you to have privacy and control over your dwelling or can be rented to generate income for you; you can keep your food longer in a refrigerator; your stocks and bonds yield some income for you – dividends from the stocks, regular interest from the bonds. Money in the form of cash in your wallet or in your checking accounts generates zero income; cash in your wallet can be lost or stolen, especially the latter if it is kept under the mattress or in a cookie jar. True story: Someone hid his money in the fireplace flue; an unexpected cold snap surprised him and he rushed and started a fire. A lot of unhealthy smoke from burning the cash spewed out of the chimney that night. (Incidentally, cash is handled by many people and can collect germs, harmful chemicals or illegal drugs along the way).

When wealth is kept in some form other than cash, it can generate income, as mentioned above. But pretty much all types of nonmonetary assets can change in value as well, sometimes upward and sometimes downward. As soon as you drive your new car out of the lot, this asset loses some of its value; the same is true of furniture. Houses rise in value during some years, such as since around 2010; but their values can fall dramatically, as in 2008-2010. The same is true of stocks; in fact, stock prices fluctuate daily, even from second to second. When your assets rise in value your wealth increases; when they fall in value your wealth falls. It should be mentioned that home prices also fluctuate, perhaps even daily, but we don't notice it because we don't put our houses on the market all the time and price them on a daily basis. In contrast, stocks are priced every second.

Chapter 6

FINANCIAL ACCOUNTING:

INCOME STATEMENT AND BALANCE SHEET

Here we introduce elements of accounting so that everyone can read a financial statement and make sense of it. The reader can construct her or his own statements to keep track of he or his financial condition. We'll go over some very simple Income Statement and Balance Sheet. The Income Statement tells you how a business or an individual has done during a given period, for corporations usually every 3 months and for most individuals once a year.

The Balance Sheet is analogous to a photograph; it indicates the financial condition of an entity at a point in time. It reflects the amount of assets and debt that a household or business has accumulated over time, such as home and furniture and mortgage for individuals, and plant and loans for businesses.

As an employee you get paid periodically (weekly or monthly, say) and at the end of the year you find out that you have earned $48,000 in salary, interest and from all other sources, from which $10,000 have been taken out as taxes, leaving $38,000 for you – this is your (net after tax) earnings. You spent $35,000 on rent, food, clothing, fuel, health care, and so on, and are left with $3,000; the $35,000 is a cost or *expense* – the cost of just being alive – and the $3,000 is your saving. These savings accumulate over time with which you buy cars, houses, furniture and so on, things that last a long time (unlike food and some clothing). These are your *gross assets*. But many of these assets, such as your furniture, cars, and house do fall in value due to wear and tear and just old age; this fall in value is called *depreciation*. But while you spend cash to buy all these assets, their depreciation does not use up cash; depreciation is merely a "book keeping" item (for most individuals you may keep track of depreciation in your mind – e.g., after one year you know in your mind that your car is worth less than one year ago). But when you repair your car, you spend cash to do so; this is a cash transaction.

The same idea applies to businesses but with additional complexities. Below is shown a simple Income Statement.

Income Statement, December 31, 2017-December 31, 2018

Sales (or Revenues)	$100
Less, Expense (Cost of Goods Sold)	60
Gross Margin	40
Less, Research & Development	4
Earnings before Depreciation	36
Less, Depreciation	6
Gross Earnings	30
Less, Tax @20%	9
Net Income	$ 21
Less, Dividends	5
Retained Earnings	$ 16

This company reports net income (earnings) of $21. But just like your situation when you figured your car had depreciated but you didn't spend any cash on depreciation, neither has this company. Its *cash flow* is actually the $21 plus the $6 in depreciation, or $27. Depreciation has the benefit of lowering the tax the company pays. Without depreciation the company would have to pay 30% on $36 of earnings before depreciation, or $10.80 (instead of $9 that it does pay). As individuals we don't get this benefit (there are exceptions, e.g., when a person owns a rental house).

Research and Development (R&D) is money spent to come up with new products, new ways of doing things to improve efficiency, to open new markets, and so on. The result of money spent on R&D, if spent well, shows up in higher earnings in the future and can last for many years. Suppose that the company wants to increase its <u>current</u> earnings. One way to do that is to cut back on R&D; the effect shows up immediately in higher earnings, but it can hurt the company's performance for years in the future. This exemplifies one way in which businesses can manipulate their earnings – there are many other ways – perhaps to cover up weak management.

Let's assume the company pays $5 in dividends. The other $16 is held in the company's accounts and it called *retained earnings*. The company can use these funds to add to its equipment or to repair its plant and so on, or just save them. Just as you would with your savings, these retained earnings increase the size of the company's assets.

Below is a simple Balance

Balance Sheet, December 31, 2018

Assets		Liabilities and Stockholders' Equity	
Current Assets		*Current Liabilities*	
(a) Cash	1,000	(j) Accounts Payable	360
(b) Accounts Receivable	300	(k) Other Current Liabilities	120
(c) Inventories	400		
(d) Total Current Assets (a)+(b)+(c)	1,700	(m) Total Current Liabilities (j)+(k)	480
Long-Term Assets		*Long-Term Labilities*	
(e) Land, Buildings, Equipment	4,000	(n) Long-term Debt	550
(f) Less accumulated depreciation	1,500	(p) Other Lon-term Liabilities (e.g. leases)	150
(g) Net Land, Building, Equipment (e)-(f)	2,500	(q) Total Long-Term Liabilities (n)+(p)	700
(h) Other Long-term Assets (e.g., Patents)	600	Total Liabilities	1,180
(i) Tot. Long-term Assets	3,100	(m)+(q) *Stockholders' Equity*	3,620
Total Assets (d+i)	**4,800**	**Total Liabilities and Stockholders' Equity**	**4,800**

Accounts Receivable are things such as sales on credit, and the buyer is expected to make cash payments in the near future on these purchases. Current Assets are those assets that can be transformed into cash within one year (such as savings accounts). Current Liabilities are debt that need to be paid off within one year (e.g., to suppliers of material). Stockholders' Equity is the value of the stock when the company initially sold stock to shareholders (this is not exactly accurate but it is close enough for our purpose), plus all the earnings not paid out as dividends over the years – what shows up as Retained Earnings in the Income Statement that have been accumulated. Note that Total Assets must necessarily be equal to Total Liabilities plus Shareholders' Equity. In theory, if you paid off all the debt the company owes (its Total Liabilities) and sold all its Total Assets, what's left goes to shareholders; that amount is $3,620.

Earnings per Share (EPS)

If you take the Net Income of $21 that appears in the Income Statement and divide it by the total number of common shares outstanding you come up with *earnings per share*, *EPS*. A company's earnings are usually not available for distribution in full to shareholders. The company needs to fund the repair of its equipment and buildings, the replacement of worn out equipment, and expansion of its production capacity. The money to cover such costs comes out of the cash generated internally or externally. The source of internal cash is usually earnings; and sometimes the firm can sell some of its assets to generate cash. The source of external funds is borrowing and the sale of additional stock. In general, a firm uses some of its earnings to cover these expenses. What's left over is called *free cash flow*, and it is free cash that is available for dividends or stock repurchases.

To better understand the concept of earnings versus free cash flow suppose that you own a house that is fully paid for. You rent out the house for $800 per month, $9,600 per year. Your real estate tax eats up $900 of this, leaving you with $8,700. The tenant pays for all utilities, and cable and internet. The $8,700 is analogous to the company earnings. But if you want to keep your house in good condition you need to make the occasional repairs (e.g., a frozen pipes or leaking roof) and regular maintenance (e.g., taking care of the lawn, cleaning the gutters); these expenditures ensure that your house keeps its value and can command a high rent. Let's say these expenses amount to $650 per year. The $8,050 (= $8,700-$650) that is left is what you can spend in any way you wish to enjoy life – this is your "free cash flow."

P/E Ratio

One measure investors use to decide whether a stock is over- or underpriced is the *price-earnings* or *P/E* ratio. This is the ratio of the current per share price of the stock divided by its earnings per share (EPS). The inverse of the P/E is earnings per share (EPS) divided by price per share. It gives you an idea of what is the percentage rate you earn on your stock.

Currently, for the S&P500 overall, the P/E ratio is around 24; the inverse of this figure is 1/24 = 4.17% so that you earn about 4.17% for each dollar invested in the S&P500. It turns out that the historical average PE ratio for the S&P500 is around 15 so that the current S&P500 is quite high, perhaps too high.

GAAP and Pro-Forma Financial Statements

When it comes to reading financial statements and financial announcements by companies a great deal of care must be exercised. U.S. companies must follow the rules established by the *Financial Accounting Standards Board (FASB)*. These rules establish what is referred to as *Generally Accepted Accounting Principles*, or *GAAP*. But companies have substantial leeway on how to treat their financial results. For example, sales of products to be delivered in the future can be booked now, regardless of delivery date or even if the sales can be cancelled. There is also a board whose job is to establish uniform rules for all companies throughout the world; this board is the *International Accounting Standards Board (IASB)*.

A game some companies play is to announce *pro-forma* financial statements. These statements can be anything the company wants to show to the public to put the management in a good light. As a rule, you should ignore these statements – they are as good as invented out of thin air.

However, many companies use what <u>academics</u> also call pro-forma statements; these are internal planning documents to help the business forecast its financial condition and needs. As internal documents, the corporation has the freedom to assume whatever is reasonable to serve its business purposes.

Chapter 7

LEVERAGE

We use leverage extensively so it is useful to cover this topic briefly. Almost everyone has used leverage at some point, sometimes unknowingly. In the world of finance, leverage means using debt in buying an asset. Leverage can be both good or bad. To see the importance of leverage, consider the amount of debt people carry. As of the second quarter of 2018, consumer credit alone amounted to $4 trillion, mortgages were $15.1 trillion, and we owed $1.1 trillion on cars. Student loans added another $1.5 trillion to the total; student loans are made to educate the borrower, that is, add to the *human capital* (an asset) of the student; this is an example of buying an asset with borrowed funds.

Most people borrow when buying a house. You find a house that you just love to own, but it costs $350,000 and all the cash you have or can get your hands on is $87,000, not nearly enough to buy the house. Your friendly (or perhaps not so friendly) banker is willing to lend you money. She asks that you put down at least 20%, which is the amount common these days, and she will lend you the rest. This means that you need to put down $70,000 – this is called your *equity* – and the banker lends you the remaining $280,000 to buy the house (let's leave aside for now the other costs that one incurs when buying a house, called "closing" costs).

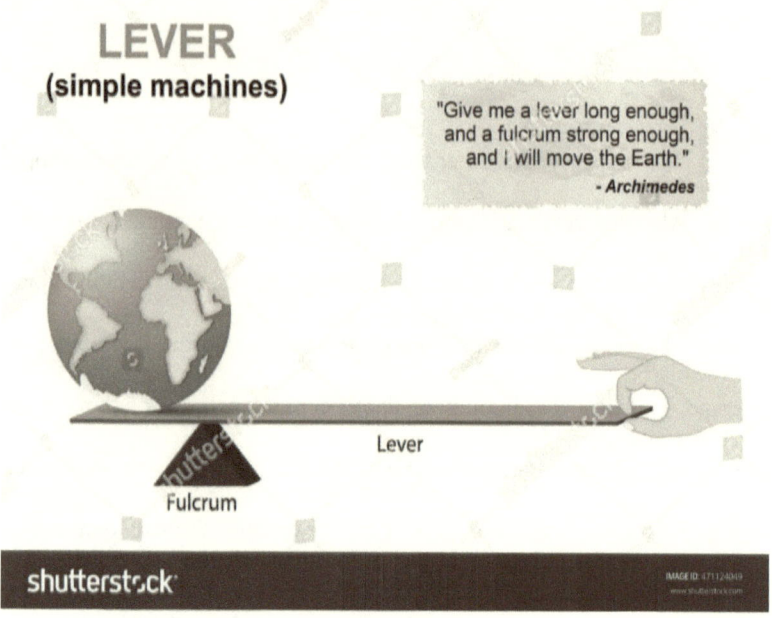

With borrowing (leverage) you can increase the amount you invest in assets

Now let's say that the value of your house rises to $395,000 in two years. Since you still owe the bank very close to $280,000 (because in the two years you have hardly paid down the loan as most of the payments you have made go to cover the interest), your equity now amounts to $115,000, the difference between the value of the house and the amount you owe to the bank. This means that you have earned a whopping 64.29% on your initial investment of $70,000. But the downside is that the value of your house may also fall, as real estate values did in 2008-2010 period. Suppose the value of your house drops to $310,000, in which case the value of your equity is now only $30,000 – a depressing loss of 57.14% on your $70,000 investment. If you had bought the house with your own funds without a loan, when the house value rose to $395,000 you would have earned only 12.86% on your initial investment, and when the house value fell to $310,000 you would have lost only 11.43%. But note that the absolute dollar values are the same whether there is borrowing or not.

This is how leverage works. It magnifies gains and losses (in percentage terms). The reason is that the loan allows you to buy a more valuable asset than if you had used only your own (limited) cash. The reason leverage has this magnifying effect is that the value of the asset changes as does the value of your equity, but the value of the loan does not. Of course, you can use leverage when you buy stocks too. You borrow money and add that to your own money to buy stocks. When the stock price goes up, the percentage gain on your stock is magnified, just like the situation with the house example discussed above. But you now know that if the stock price falls, your losses are multiplied as well. Here's an example. You have $900 and you borrow $400 at an interest of 4% per year to buy 100 GE shares at $13 each. After one year the share price rises by $1.30 each, a 10% rise, and you can sell your shares for $1,430 for a gain of $130. You pay back the $400 loan plus $16 in interest, leaving you with $1,014; this is a 12.67% return on your $900 investment, much higher than the 10% increase in the price of the stock. However, had the stock price fallen by 10% to $11.70, your loss would have been greater than 10% –

you would have lost 16.22% since you had to repay the loan plus interest of $416. While the value of the stock can change, the value of the loan plus interest does not.

Instead of borrowing money to buy a stock or an asset, you can use options and futures. Futures are used widely to take positions in assets. Both options and futures are a means to leverage one's acquisition of assets (these securities will be discussed in a later chapter).

Keep in mind that when you buy a house you also incur closing costs of something like $8,000 (taxes, insurance, and other costs) – which you can afford since you have $87,000 cash. Once you take these additional costs into account the returns change but you can see what is involved in leverage.

Now that we are on the issue of debt, we might as well discuss the repayment of the loan. The bank requires regular interest payments and a gradual repayment of the *principal* $280,000 (called *amortization* of the loan). If the rate of interest is 4.0% and the loan is repaid in 30 years, then your total monthly payment, which includes loan pay-down and the interest, will be $1,336.76 per month. The loan is amortized gradually, every month over 30 years. In the early months most of the $1,336.763 goes toward interest payments since you owe $280,000; in the first month close to $940 of your payment goes to cover the interest on the loan, so only about $403 is to pay off the loan. Toward the end of the loan period, say at the beginning of year 29, most of the $1,336.76 payment covers the loan, and little interest is paid – something like $125 in interest. This is because you have almost paid off the entire $280,000 (actually, you still owe about $38,000) so the house is nearly all yours – congratulations! The loan is *fully amortized* when you make you last payment.

You have probably experienced yourself or know somebody who bought a car on credit to be paid off in five years. After 3 or 4 payments you decide to pay off the loan on the car; when you go to the bank to pay off the loan you discover that you owe the bank nearly as much as the borrowed amount. That is again because the early payments cover mainly the interest and little of the original value of the loan (called the *principal*).

Leverage's impact on businesses is exactly the same as the examples given here. Leverage can boost a company's earnings when times are good but that comes at a price. When business conditions deteriorate, leverage becomes very burdensome. A highly-leveraged company's earnings are subject to greater volatility than the earnings of less-leveraged company. In other words, the more-leveraged company's earnings are riskier. Accordingly, such a company's shares are riskier as well and this riskiness is reflected in the stock price. Precisely because leverage increases earnings volatility, companies with steadier sales and profits are the ones with high leverage. Thus, we find utilities carry higher debt loads than equipment makers.

Taxes play a role here too. For businesses, all the interest they pay is deductible as an expense so interest reduces tax on income. In a real sense, the exemption of interest from income is a subsidy on interest, increasing the incentive to borrow. The same applies to individuals, except that there is a limit on how much interest can be used by individuals to decrease their tax liabilities.

Chapter 8

INTEREST RATE, DIVIDEND, AND RATE OF RETURN

Interest is paid on loans and *dividends* are paid on stocks. Loans are often in the form of bonds and bonds pay the bondholder interest, usually every six months. Stocks, if they are dividend-paying, pay the shareholder a dividend every three months.

Interest Rate

Interest is what you earn when you lend funds to others. An example is the interest you receive on your *savings* account (also called *time* deposit) at a bank. You deposit $300 in a savings account and the bank pays you $7.50 a year on these funds; the $7.50 is the interest. Your friend has $400 in a savings account at a different bank and receives $9.00 in interest a year and encourages you to switch your savings to her bank. Should you? After all she has more funds in her account than you do so your $7.50 and her $9.00 may not be comparable. To make a correct comparison, you want to use what is referred to as interest *rate*, which asks how much interest you get per each $100.00 in your account (better yet, interest per $1.00). Your bank pays $2.50 in interest per $100 in deposit, your friend's pays $2.25 in interest per $100 in deposit. Now you have the answer: you should keep your account with your current bank and she should switch to your bank. These figures are obtained by dividing the interest by the size of the deposit: $7.50 divided by $300, and $9.00 divided by $400. If we drop the "$" sign from $2.50 and $2.25, and add the "%" sign after those numbers we get 2.50% and 2.25%, respectively – these are called *rates* of interest. Interest rates are usually expressed in "percentage terms on a per year" basis. In our examples, they are 2.50% per year and 2.25% per year, respectively.

There are a vast number of interest rates, ranging from nearly zero (sometimes even negative) to relatively high figures, perhaps as high as 40% or even higher. A loan shark may charge an interest rate of "only" 4% per week; to annualize this rate an easy way is to multiply the 4% by 52 weeks per year – which gives you 208%. Actually, the correct rate of interest of 4% per week is substantially higher at 669% per year! To obtain 669% we have to calculate what is called *compound* interest.

Negative Interest Rate

Most people, even some trained economists, assume that interest rates can only be positive. The reasoning used is that "why should I lend you $100 and after one year get back the $100 without anything added to it. I might as well keep the $100 in my wallet or my bank – without risking getting my money back." The argument for the absence of negative interest rate is even stronger according to this view since negative interest means that someone lends you $100 but get back less, say, $98. Put another way, he lends you $100 but also pays you $2 so that you would borrow from him – that sounds absurd, doesn't it? This logic led many economists to argue that interest rates could not be negative, the so-called "zero lower bound" rate.

But the rate of interest does not have to be positive. Consider the situation where you are in the business of selling some highly perishable product, such as fresh fish, and lack refrigeration or other means to prevent spoilage (this is in fact a condition in which small fishermen find themselves in many places in Africa, Asia, and Latin America). You would be willing to give the product to someone who promises to pay you back in kind in the future, but a lesser quantity that he receives. This is a better deal than lose the product entirely to spoilage. So, in principle, interest rates can be negative. In the mid-2010s some interest rates did become negative in several countries (e.g., Switzerland, Japan, Germany). With a negative interest, as shown above, the borrower pays back less than she borrows. Why would you lend money at a negative rate? It could be that you have so much money that it becomes costly and burdensome to keep it with you. For instance, you may need to rent a safety deposit box (and pay a fee) in a bank to safeguard your cash; it may be cheaper to "lend" it to a trustworthy individual (say, a central bank) at a negative interest rate.

Simple Interest

Simple interest is what you are getting on your savings account. The bank pays you $7.50 on your $300 deposit or 2.50% per year, year after year, as long as you keep your money at that bank. What you have in your savings account stays constant at $300 year after year.

Compound Interest

Suppose a bank offers you the following deal. Deposit $300.00 in your savings account as before but with this difference: if you leave your money in that account for 2 years and do not withdraw the original deposit (the *principal*) nor the interest earned, then the bank will pay interest on the earned interest that you did not withdraw. Not only will you earn 2.50% on the principal but 2.50% on the interest of $7.50.

Let's see how does this work. At the end of the year 1 you earn 2.50% on $300, which is $7.50. Now you start year 2 with $307.50. At the end of the year 2, you will have $307.50 plus the 2.50% interest on $307.50, or $7.6875, for a total of $315.1875. Another way of looking at this is this: you earn 7.50 in each of two years on the original $300 for a total of $15.00; you also earn 2.50% on the $7.50 that you left in the bank in year 1– that amounts to $7.50 × 2.50% = $0.1875. Note that you earn interest on the principal $300 for two years, but for only one year on the $7.50 interest, because the $7.50 is in your account for just one year. This is the power of compounding. If you leave your $300 in the bank and let all interests that you earn stay in your account and earn the same 2.50%, after 30 years you end up with $629.27, which is your original $300 plus an additional $329.27 in interest. The interest earned exceeds your initial deposit; not bad at all.

What all this means for you as a saver is that the earlier you start saving and the more you save, the wealthier you will be when you are ready to retire. Postpone your enjoyment of owning things (expensive clothes, nice appliances and furniture, that super-duper pickup truck, that fancy game room, and so on) when you are young in exchange for these same things and a lot more 15-20 year down the road. The question for you is: can you control your urges now for the sake of a better, much better, future? Nobody can decide this for you. It is all a matter of personal taste – <u>your</u> taste and preferences.

Return on Investment

The $300 you deposited in your savings account is *investment*. As we will see, investment can take many forms. When you invest, you want to know how much you get back in return; that is, what is the *return* on your investment? At 2.50% per year, after one year your return on $300 is $7.50. If you leave the interest to earn more interest, after two years your return is $15.188, after three years you return will be $26.067, and so forth.

Time	0	1	2	3
Return ($)	0	7.50	15.188	26.067
Total ($)	300	307.50	315.188	326.067

Consider the situation after 2 years, when your total (compound) return is $15.188. Suppose that your friend also deposits $300 in a savings account and earns 2.50% on her account but closes her account after 1 year, receiving her original $300 plus the interest of $7.50. Who has earned more? You have, of course. But you left your money in the bank for two years while your friend left her money in the account for only one year. There is something wrong here: we have not taken into account the length of time you have left your funds in the bank compared to your friend. To make the correct comparison we have to take into account the length of time funds sit in a bank earning interest. In this case, you are both earning $7.50 per year on your $300.

What if your friend had deposited $400? And what if her bank paid an interest rate of 3.00%? The numbers would be different and we couldn't make appropriate decisions. To resolve all these complexities, we use *rate* of return, instead of just "return". Rate of return applies to return earned in *one* year on $100. For you the rate of return on your deposit of $300 is 2.50% per year; for your friend, the rate of return on $400 is 3.00% per year – she has the better deal.

Dividend

On savings accounts, banks *promise* to pay you a fixed amount each year. It is a promise because, under certain conditions, if the bank goes under the interest may not be paid (and you might even lose the principal). Among those conditions is how much you have in your savings account and whether it is insured by the government. Currently, an account in a U.S. depository institution is insured up to $250,000. The insurance is by the federal government's FDIC (Federal Deposit Insurance Corporation).

You can also invest your savings in stocks. Stocks are issued by *corporations* (i.e., companies) and represent ownership in the business a corporation is in. You become a *stockholder* (or *shareholder*); this means that you own a part of the company. The funds that are left after the corporation pays its taxes, workers, suppliers of material and equipment, and creditors, are referred to as its profits and belong to the shareholders. The company can decide to distribute some or all (or none) of these profits to its shareholders. These distributed funds are called *dividends*. Unlike interest, dividends are not fixed and are usually paid every quarter – and they can vary from quarter to quarter. If you compare the dividend to the price of the stock on any particular day, you obtain what is called the dividend *yield*. At the time of this writing the dividend General Electric (GE) pays is $0.12 per quarter so the annual dividend is $0.48. Since GE's stock price is $12.83, its *dividend yield* is calculated by dividing the annual dividend of $0.48 by its current price of $12.83, which is $0.48/$12.83 = 0.0374 or 3.74%.

Unlike your savings account whose principal does not change (if you keep withdrawing only the interest earned), the stock prices change almost every second – whether or not you get paid dividends.

Capital Gain

When you put $300 in your savings account, you could withdraw the $7.50 interest at the end of year. If you leave your funds (the principal) in your account, you will always have $300 that you could withdraw at the appropriate time. With stocks it is different. As mentioned earlier the price of a share rises and falls. The difference between the original price that you paid and the price at any time is call *capital gain* or *capital loss*. The capital gain is added to the profit you make when you sell the stock; capital loss, of course, deducts from your profit – that is, results in loss. If the stock pays dividends as well, then you must add the dividends to your capital gain (or capital loss) to compute your return. If you bought GE's share for $12.15 one year ago and the current price is $12.83, your capital gain is $12.83 - $12.15 = $0.68; your total return is therefore $0.48 + $0.68 = $1.16. The rate of return on this investment is $1.16/$12.15 = 0.09547 or 9.547%.

Long Term and Short Term Interest Rates

You can deposit your money with a bank and agree not to withdraw your funds for one year; usually banks allow you to break the agreement and take your funds out but pay a penalty, most often in the form of reduced interest. You can also agree to give your money to the bank and not touch it for, say, five years. Or you can lend your money to the U.S. government (actually you would give it to the U.S. Treasury Department) and not touch it for ten or even 20 years. The interest rates on all these various lending alternatives vary for many reasons, one important of which is the length of time you promise not to want your money back sooner than agreed upon.

In all these cases, you don't really give your money away – you just *lend* your money, which is why it is called a *loan*. In exchange, the borrower gives you some document that proves he/she/it has borrowed a certain sum from you. This document is called a *bond*. We'll return to bonds shortly and discuss them in more detail. For now, it should be understood that depending on the length of time you lend your money, the interest rate may vary. In most situations, the longer is the time the loan is made for the higher is the rate of interest on the loan. Thus, when you promise not to take out the money in your savings account for two years you earn a higher interest than if you left your money in your account for only one year. A bank that offers 2.3% on a one-year deposit, may pay 2.5% on a two-year account, and 2.9% on a three-year deposit. (These are actual rates paid on Certificates of Deposit, or CDs, as of late June 2018; CDs are a form of bonds issued by banks).

Among the reasons why interest rates on longer-term loans are higher than on shorter-term loans is that you have your money tied up for longer period. You don't have access to it in case you need it yourself for an emergency or for a great deal that shows up unexpectedly. Another reason is that you have agreed to a certain interest rate for several years and if interest rates rise across the board, you lose the opportunity to lend your funds at a higher rate. At the same time, if rates fall you benefit from having a longer-term agreement. There are other reasons for variations for loans of different durations, but the explanations offered here are sufficient to understand what's going on in the market for loans (bonds).

Chapter 9

RISK AND RETURN

One of the best understood principles in economics is that investment encompasses risk and to earn higher return on investment one assumes more risk. The important thing to keep in mind is that all investments, except for less than a handful of them, are risky. The exceptions are U.S. Treasury, German government, Japanese government and Swiss government short-term (less than one year) bonds. Whenever you consider an investment's return it is imperative that you also consider its risk. Risk and return are inseparable, they go hand-in-hand – they share the same DNA.

Risk and Return are twins, more like Siamese Twins, that not even the most skilled surgeon – or fund manager – can separate them.

Any time someone mentions return, inquire about the associated risk. When at a cocktail party a guest brags about the return he earned on his latest investment, immediately think how much risk he accepted in return (assuming he is not just making up stories to keep the party warm); you are likely to be shocked by the amount of risk he took.

What is Risk?

Among the factors that help determine a stock's price is *risk*. We all know what risk is, right? It is something bad, something to avoid. If you drive at 105 miles per hour, you risk getting caught by the highway patrol and receive a hefty fine; if you are lucky (!) no cop bothers to try to catch you but you may have a massive accident and end up in the hospital. Driving at high speed is risky and for this reason the vast majority of people drive at reasonable speeds. But the flip side of driving fast is the likelihood of getting to your destination sooner – and you will avoid hearing the perennial question "are we there yet?" We have the same idea in investment: risk has a downside as well as an upside. And studies support the view that people in general, and investors in particular, dislike risk; professionals refer to this as *risk aversion*. Neuroscientists tell us that risk aversion is part and parcel of the human psyche, a consequence of evolution and adaptation.

Remember the famous statement of Donald Rumsfeld's? Here it is (paraphrased): there are known knowns, there are known *un*knowns and there are *un*known *un*knowns. Risk is the known unknown. Just in case, you are interested, the economist Frank Knight distinguished between risk and "uncertainty" decades ago. To Knight, uncertainty is the unknown unknown.

It should be added that those very people who are risk averse in their investments do engage in risk-taking activities as well. Observe the millions (billions?) of people who love gambling. This includes paying to play games in casinos where on average the gambler must lose; that's how casinos make money. And millions (billions?) buy lottery tickets; again, the issuer makes money by selling lottery tickets; after winners are paid their prizes, money is left over to fund various activities. Lotteries are a losing proposition for the buyer. True, sometimes the top prize is in the hundreds of millions of dollars, but the likelihood of winning the top prize is less than the probability of getting hit by lightning three times within three days in mid-July in your favorite bar in the middle of the Arabian desert.

Types of Risk: Market and Specific

There are two genres of risk. One is related to the overall economy or the investment market in its entirety, and it is called *market risk* (also called *systematic* or *undiversifiable*). The other relates to the specific investment or asset, and it is called *specific risk* (sometimes referred to as *idiosyncratic* or *diversifiable*).

When the stock market as a whole rises, most stocks rise with it as well and when the stock market as whole falls so do most stocks. When the housing market is on a roll, your house value rises too and when the housing market collapses, as it did in 2008-2010, most everybody's home prices decline as well. And there isn't much one can do when things like that happen. The value of your investment moves up and down with what is going on in the broader market or the economy; your investment is at the mercy of the "market".

But some investments are riskier than others due to the nature of the asset itself. A lottery ticket is very risky: there is one chance in tens or even hundreds of millions to win the top prize. The value of a new business (a *startup*) is highly uncertain and, therefore, that business is quite risky. Searching for treasures contained in a shipwreck in the middle of the Atlantic Ocean is very risky: you may find nothing after spending years and millions of dollars, but you may also find treasures worth hundreds of millions of dollars, irrespective of how the stock market is doing or whether the economy is growing or contracting. These are examples of risk associated with the particular investment.

Or consider drilling for crude oil. Major oil companies long ago learned that of all the onshore wells they drill something like one-quarter to one-third of the wells produce economically viable oil. Each well is different; some must be drilled deep, some shallower; some need to be drilled horizontally; some need to have water pumped in them to extract the oil. As a result, some wells are cheaper to extract oil from, and some are dry. All these characteristics of individual wells constitute specific risk. If you invest in only one well, you can lose all your money or make lots of money. But if you spread your money on 200 wells, there is an extremely high likelihood that you will a <u>reasonable</u> amount of money: some 50 of these wells will produce oil for you. This is the result of *diversification*; the "good" wells cover the loss of "bad" wells and some. This is precisely how major oil companies make money – by drilling lots of wells (thousands of wells are drilled every year). While 70%-75%of these wells are dry, the remainder do produce oil. This is like tossing a fair coin numerous times; on average you will end up with heads close to one-half the time.

There are two types of risks associated with a stock. The specific risk is particular to the company. Each company is different along various dimensions: industry, management philosophy and competence, size and market share, product type, pricing power, technology, etc. But all stocks tend to respond to the overall stock market behavior, some by little, some by a lot, and some (few) by moving in the opposite direction. If you invest in a well-diversified portfolio – that is, in a fairly large number of stocks in different industries – the specific risks are pretty much eliminated. What's left is the market risk – the risk that all stocks bear because of fluctuations in the overall market. But if you invest in only one stock, you will bear both types of risk – the specific as well as the market.

Compensation for Taking Risk

The economy compensates the investor for only the market risk. Why? Because the economy compensates people for incurring the cost of doing something. You get paid wages for working because the cost of work to you is the leisure time you give up. You are paid for the apples you sell to me because you could have sold them to your friend; I have to compensate you for the money you gave up by not selling the apples to him. Diversification of a portfolio – which eliminates specific risk – is costless and, therefore, accepting specific risk is not rewarded. Instead of spending all your money to invest in 1,000 shares of only one company, you can buy shares in a mutual fund that invests in all the publicly traded companies (more realistically, the fund may invest in a portfolio that replicates the overall market); this means that you can eliminate specific risk without incurring any cost.

Benefits of Diversification

Here's how diversification works. Consider a situation where the overall stock market is not changing. Because of the peculiarities of each company, on any particular day the stocks of some companies rise by a lot, some by a little, some fall by a lot, and some by a little. For example, if there is an extended period of rain many people buy umbrellas and raincoats, but few buy ice-cream and cold drinks. The stocks of cold-weather product companies rise and those of warm-weather product companies fall. If you own stocks in both industries, your portfolio is protected against the vagaries of the weather; your portfolio has diversified away the specific risk. It is precisely this way that diversification of a portfolio purges specific risk – that is why specific risk is often referred to as "diversifiable" risk. Unfortunately, market risk cannot be diversified away: all stocks are subject to it; and all <u>assets</u> are affected by it. You can <u>reduce</u> the magnitude of market risk by diversifying across assets (e.g., by investing in real estate, commodities, stocks and bonds) and across national borders, but market risk is enduring. The trick to diversification is the "correlation" between the returns of different asset classes, as shown in the table below for the case of two assets X and Y:

Assets	Correlation			
X and Y	High Positive	Low Positive	Low Negative	High Negative
Diversification Value	Low	High	Higher	Highest

Correlation measures the association of the return on one asset with the return on another. If the correlation is zero it means that the two returns are totally unrelated: the return on the first asset can go up while the return on the second can remain unchanged, rise or fall. If the correlation is negative, when the return on the first asset rises, the return on the second falls. With a positive correlation, the rise in the return on the first is accompanied with the rise in the second asset.

In the above table, if the correlation of returns on assets (or stocks) X and Y is high, the returns move up and down together and one doesn't gain much by having both X and Y in one's portfolio. In contrast, if when the return on X rises when the return on Y falls, and vice versa, then diversification works well.

Alpha and Beta

Fund managers often talk about *alpha* and *beta*; for many fund managers, their compensation is closely tied to these Greek letters (especially, alpha). The riskiness of a stock derives from two sources: when the overall market's return changes so does the return on all stocks (this due to the systematic component of risk), but the return on a particular stock can change due to the specific nature of the company that stock represents, even if the market is completely stable (this is due to the idiosyncratic component of risk). The total return on a stock is determined by the sum of the two risks, systematic and idiosyncratic. Beta measures the sensitivity of a security's return to the market's return, the systematic component. The part of a stock's return that is not explained by beta is called "alpha". Both beta and alpha can range between negative and positive numbers.

Pacific Gas and Electric (PCG) has beta = - 0.4, Apple (AAPL) has beta = +1.1, and General Motors (GM) has beta = +1.3. Beta tells you by what percentage should the return on a stock change when the overall market changes by 1 percent. If the market return rises by 1%, PCG's return is expected to fall by 0.4%, that of AAPL to rise by 1.1% and that of GM to rise by 1.3%. Suppose that when the market's return rises by 1% it is observed that GM's return rises by 2.0% and AAPL's return rises by 0.5%. This would mean that alpha for GM is 2.0 -1.3 = 0.7 and AAPL's alpha is 0.5 -1.1= - 0.6. These alphas suggest that GM beats the market and AAPL falls short. Investors and fund managers try their best to avoid stocks and portfolios with negative alpha, seeking those with positive alpha. Alpha, in a sense, measures the skill of the investor in identifying stocks whose returns exceed the market return on a risk-adjusted basis. Someone who invests in the market as a whole need not worry about alphas and betas – the overall market's beta is 1: when the market return changes by 1%, the market return changes by 1% !

The concepts of alpha and beta are based on a model to explain stock returns. This is the 1960s Capital Asset Pricing Model (CAPM, read as "Capem"). Empirically, it doesn't do a good job and alternatives have been proposed. Conceptually, however, the CAPM is a useful.

Alpha and beta are statistical estimates. As such, their estimated values can change as the period during which their values are measured changes. Accordingly, one set of estimates can differ from the set obtained during a different period. The betas used here are estimated using returns over 2014-2018 and are used for illustration purposes.

Chapter 10

SECURITIES

In an economy there are many ways to hold wealth. Wealth is held in some sort of asset. Some assets are highly *liquid*, others not so. An asset is said to be liquid if it can be sold easily and readily at its "true" market value. Currency is the most liquid of assets: you can exchange $1 for $1 at the bat of an eye. A diamond ring that you bought for $2,000, may fetch only $1,200 if you wanted to sell it without waiting long; this ring is far less liquid than currency. A house may take three months to sell, even if it is sold for the true market price; the house is also less liquid than cash. A notch less liquid than cash are various securities.

Real Assets and Financial Assets

Real assets determine the productive capacity of a country and are owned by its people. Of course, some individuals may own a larger share of these assets than others. These assets include land, buildings, knowledge and equipment that have the capacity to produce goods and services.

Financial assets are instruments by means of which individuals hold their claims on real assets. Securities are financial assets and consist of *currency* (cash) and three broad groups: *stocks, bonds,* and *derivatives*. Securities are sheets of papers or computer digital entries, and they are not producers of goods and service. They are claims to the income real assets provide or claims on income from the government. The ultimate value of a security is an asset that itself can create value, such as a business, a house, a factory, an invention, a computer code, a copyright, a trademark, or a patent.

Financial assets result from the need to finance the acquisition of real assets. For example, if a company wants to build a plant to produce fans it needs to finance the plant. It can sell a portion of the ownership to investors to obtain the needed funds. Or consider a company that wants to employ code writers to develop a computerized investment program, but it is short of funds to complete the code. It can sell part of the business by selling shares, thus obtaining the money to fund the project. Alternatively, the company can borrow the funds from the investors and, as proof of the loan, the company issues bonds to them. In either case, the stocks and bonds are claims on the income generated by the real assets of the company.

Since financial assets themselves are not productive, why do they exist? Financial assets make the market and the economy work more smoothly. They allow the transfer of claims work efficiently (that is, easily and at low cost).

Economic Efficiency of Financial Assets and Markets

Once securities were invented, financial markets came into existence. Securities are bought and sold in these markets, and their prices are determined therein. These prices reflect the "collective estimation" of the productive capacity and profitability of the real assets those securities represent. The higher prices of the stock of a company makes it easier for the firm to raise funds to purchase additional capacity, both equipment and workers. This is how resources are allocated to their best use in a modern economy. Of course, at times resources go to wasteful ventures or some useful projects are underfunded. But this is because we don't know with certainty what products or services will be needed and useful in the future.

By selling securities to investors, the owners of a company give up partial ownership, but they also pass part of the "risk" of the business to shareholders and bondholders. Those individuals who are the most risk tolerant will allocate a larger portion of their savings to stock (and to the stocks of the riskier businesses). Those with less taste for risk will invest in bonds (and the least risky bonds, such as the U.S. Treasury securities, particularly the shorter-term ones).

Financial assets allow individuals to better plan their *consumption timing*. Younger people earn less than they want or need to spend. For example, a college student earns much less than he needs to finance his education. He can rely on financial markets to help him out – e.g., through some kind of loan, such as government-subsidized or government guaranteed loans. At the height of her earning capacity, when her income is higher than her expenses, a manager can save for her retirement. She does so by buying various securities which, in turn, represent real assets. These assets entitle her to the income they generate.

Investing in securities permits the investors to remove themselves from the operations of the company. This is referred to as the *separation of ownership and management.* The protect themselves against mismanagement, shareholders elect a *board of directors* (BOD) to represent them. The board, in turn, selects the top managers of the company. The board is supposed to supervise the management to ensure that they work for the benefit of the shareholders. One mechanism used for this supervision is the "audit" by outside auditors.

But this setup leads to a potential problem: The *agency problem.* In reality many, if not most companies, end up with top managers who in effect select the members of the BOD instead of the board selecting the managers, in contradiction to the companies own rules.

Like most of us, managers have the incentive to lead the good life and make as much money as possible. Having a nice office, a company jet, etc., are very important to managers and they may waste shareholder money on things like that. Managers are the shareholders' "agents" whose incentives may be in conflict with the incentives of the shareholders, the "principals". Such conflicts abound in the economy. Your realtor wants to sell your house as fast as possible so that he can list and sell another house. If he sells your house for an extra $5,000 he ends up perhaps with an extra $150 (3% of the extra $5,000) but if he can sell another house for $400,000 he collects $12,000. Here you, as principal, lose out because your incentive and your agent's are not aligned. Interestingly, studies show that realtors get significantly higher prices for the properties they own themselves than other people's properties, even when the properties are pretty much alike in all respects.

    Mechanisms have developed to mitigate the agency problem in the corporate world. The threat of takeovers is one. A proxy fight through which the BOD and management are changed is a useful tool. But proxy fights are seldom effective. Often management's compensation is tied to the performance of the company, for example, to the company's net income. But net income can be, and has been, manipulated for the benefit of the management. To illustrate, the telecom firm WorldCom overstated its profits by around $4 billion. Enron moved its debt to "special-purpose entities" to make its balance sheet seem stronger. Many other companies have manipulated their financial statements, including Rite-Aid, and Qwest. It should be added that in recent years company BODs have become more responsible and appear to be more supportive of shareholder interests. Fewer CEOs are nowadays are simultaneously BOD chairs, tending to make the BODs somewhat more independent of the management. On the other hand, management compensations have shot up and poor or unethical managers have in recent years been allowed to retire on eye-popping pensions.

Securities Regulation

In modern economies securities are heavily regulated. In the United States, the issuance and trading of securities are regulated by a myriad of laws. The most important of these laws are the *Securities Act of 1933* and the *Securities Exchange Act of 1934*. The 1933 Act establishes criteria for issuing new securities, such as disclosure of relevant information. This Act requires that new issues to be registered and a prospectus be supplied that details the financial prospects of the business.

The 1934 Act establishes the *Securities and Exchange Commission* (SEC) to administer the Securities Act provisions. Basically, the 1934 Act deals with already issued securities. It requires the periodic provision of financial information by companies that have already issued securities. The SEC is empowered to regulated securities exchanges, trading, brokers and dealers.

The SEC shares responsibility with other regulatory agencies. The Federal Reserve (the Fed) has overall responsibility for the health and functioning of the U.S. financial markets. In that role the Fed regulates bank lending to security market participants and determines margin requirements on stocks and stock options. The Commodity Futures Trading Commission (CFTC) regulates the futures markets.

In terms of investor protection, the Securities Investor Protection Act of 1970 established the Securities Investor Protection Corporation (SIPC) to insure brokerage accounts up to $500,000 if the brokerage firm fails. SIPC is financed by an insurance premium paid by the brokerage company.

The Financial Stability Oversight Council (FSOC) created by the Dodd-Frank Wall Street Reform and Consumer Protection Act of 2010 in reaction to the 2008 financial crisis. The FSOC's main role is to coordinate key financial regulators.

In addition to federal laws and regulations, state laws too play a role in regulating securities trading. These laws are known as *blue sky* laws because they aim to give investors greater transparency.

There is considerable self-regulation in the securities market. The *Financial Industry Regulatory Authority* (FINRA) is the most influential overseer. It mission is to foster market integrity and the protection of investors.

Chapter 11

STOCKS

A stock represents a share of ownership in a corporation; therefore, a stock is often referred to as a *share*. A corporation is treated as almost a person under the laws of the United States; it can buy and sell property, can sue and be sued, has freedom of speech (it can, for example, contribute money to political candidates or various causes). The shareholder is not responsible for the acts of the corporation nor its liabilities. In principle, shareholders elect a board of directors who in turn hires the management of the company; the management of the company is supposed to run the business for the benefit of its shareholders. Many company managers pay lip service to shareholders interests and, in most situations, it is management that selects the members of the board rather the other way around. So, it is important for shareholders to invest in companies who have shareholder interests as a priority.

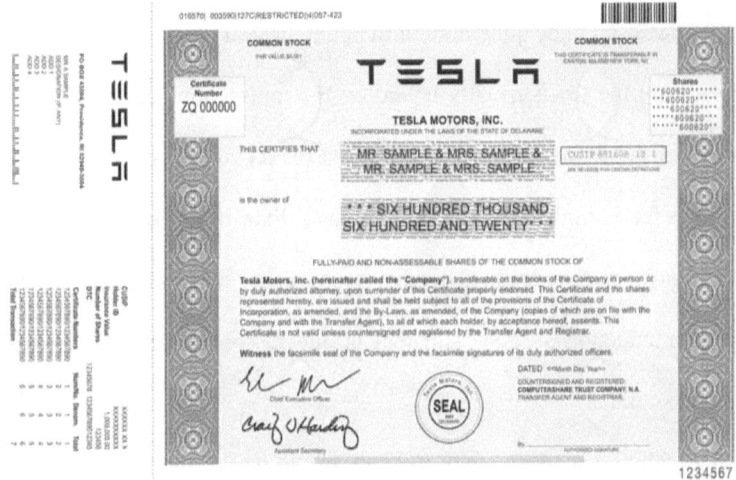

Tesla Motors Stock Certificate

Stock Market

If you decide to own the stock of a public company you have to buy it from someone who owns it and is willing to sell it. Like most other things one buys or sells, you go through a broker or a dealer whose job is to match buyers and sellers. There is a central market (actually several markets) for stocks and the broker tries to find sellers of the stock you are interested in. It turns out that to find sellers (or buyers) is not that difficult because there are large brokerage companies whose job is to make sure that you can always buy or sell stocks. They are called *market makers* and stand to buy and sell stocks of specific companies. You find a broker and tell her how many shares you want and at what price; she contacts a market maker and quotes him your price and if he finds the price attractive the transaction takes place. These intermediaries make money by charging a very small fee (the fee used to be quite high until about 30 years ago but it is minimal these days); the fee is usually levied on the transaction regardless of the number of shares involved – for example, a flat fee of $5 – so on a per share basis the fee is higher if you buy one share than if you buy 100 shares. These days transactions generally take place electronically via the telecommunication systems and that is one reason brokerage fees have dropped so much.

There are many stock markets in the world, the most important being the New York Stock Exchange (NYSE) in New York. Other important stock markets include the London, Frankfurt, Paris, Shanghai, Tokyo, and Hong Kong markets. As a result of the existence of so many exchange markets, you can buy and sell stock 24 hours a day by going through one of these markets.

Stock Market Indexes

You may be interested in how a particular stock, such as the stock of General Electric or Amazon, is doing; you can look the stock up in the newspaper (not all newspapers report the prices of all the stocks) or online via the internet or even call a stock broker. On the other hand, like most other people you may be interested in how the overall stock market is doing. For this information you look up the three major stock indexes for the U.S: the Dow-Jones Industrial Average (DJIA), the Standard & Poor's

500 (S&P500), and the Nasdaq. These are called *stock market indexes* and are reported regularly by most media, especially business newspapers (e.g., the Wall Street Journal and the New York Times Business Section) and TV channels (e.g., Bloomberg, CNBC, and Fox).

The most popular is the DJIA which reports how the "average" stock of 30 large industrial corporations is doing. Most investors prefer the S&P500 which reports the "average" value of the stocks of the 500 largest U.S.-based corporations, largest by stock market value. The Nasdaq index reports the average of 100 largest U.S. and international companies, also by stock market value, listed on the Nasdaq market; the Nasdaq consists mostly of hi-tech, biotechnology, and wholesale and retail companies. There is also a market index which covers a wider range of companies by both lines of business and size; it is the Wilshire 5000. It included approximately 5,000 companies when it was launched in the mid-1970s, but it includes around 3,800 listed companies currently. As of this writing, the DJIA stood at around 24,239.85, the S&P500 stood at 2,714.21 and the Nasdaq stood at 7,497.96. They were down respectively by 43.26, 7.76, and 58.27 points from the prior day's closing levels. The Wilshire 5000 index stood at 28,389.16, down by 105.05 points on the day.

Not all businesses are included in the stock market indexes; to be included the company must be *listed* in one of the markets. To be listed, the company must meet certain criteria, such as being examined ("audited") by licensed accounting firms and have positive "net worth"; each of the stock markets specifies its own conditions for listing.

The value of a stock market index changes by the second as any one of the stocks included in that index changes. But any one of the companies include in the DJIA has an outsized impact on the DJIA index since only 30 companies are included in the index.

Common Stocks, Preferred Stocks

When it comes to stocks, there are two broad categories of stocks. We have *common* shares and *preferred* shares. There are two main differences between them. Dividends on preferred stock are generally fixed – which makes preferred shares somewhat similar to infinite-maturity bonds – whereas dividends on common stock are decided by the board of directors every quarter, and it can vary or even be omitted. But if a dividend on preferred stock is skipped, then the company usually cannot pay a dividend on its common stock either; and when the preferred shares' dividends are omitted, common shares cannot receive dividends unless and until all the missed preferred dividends are paid (this is true if the preferred shares are *cumulative*, which is often the case). But keep in mind that like most everything else in finance, there are all sorts of variations in preferred stock issues.

Return to Stocks

So how well stocks have done in the past? Here are two diagrams, both depicting the performance of the stocks in the S&P500 index. They show the *total* return on these stocks (recall that total return includes the sum of dividends and capital gain). The first diagram shows the accumulated return: what $100 invested in these stocks in the past, along with their dividends, would be worth today. The value of the index was 255.52 in January 1928 and it is today 2,714.12, or almost 11 times higher (actually 10.62 times higher), a growth of just about 2.7% per year. Therefore, if your parents had invested $100 for you in the stock market in 1928, you would have $1,062 as of this writing. But notice that January 1928 was some 18 months before the onset of the Great Depression that started in September of 1929.

Cumulative Total Return on Stocks included in the Standard & Poor's 500

Source: www.macrotrends.net

The stock market dropped from its peak of 439 in September of 1929 to a low of 82 by May of 1932 – i.e., it lost 80 per cent of its value. The market did not reach its 1929 peak for nearly forty years, until June 1956. Many people lost everything they owned and died prematurely due to stress; despite what you may have heard, very few people jumped to their death out of their high-rise building windows. But what if you started investing in the stock market in late 1949 – after the second World War (WWII). The value of the S&P500 index stood at 160.89 then; this means your stocks would be worth 16.87 times more by now, an annual total rate of return of around 4.2%. If you started your investment in stocks in July 1982, right after the recession of the late 1980s when the index stood at 276.29, your stocks would be worth 9.82 times more valuable, for an annual total rate of return of about 6.7%. So, returns on stocks have been higher in recent years as compared to the earlier decades of the twentieth century. However, in a ten-year period ended in March 2018, stocks returned a total of a shade less than 5.8% per year; some of this lower return is due to the dismal performance of stocks during the Great Recession of 2008.

The second diagram represents the total returns for each year since 1928. For example, the market dropped a frightening 47% in 1931 in the depth of the Great Depression, but recovered a huge 46.5% just two years

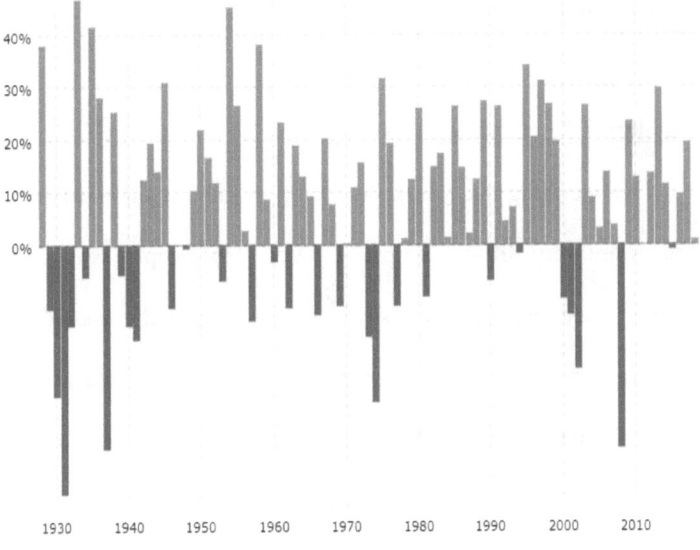

Annual Returns on Standard & Poor's 500 stocks, 1928-2107

Source: www.macrotrends.net

later in 1933. The market fell a scary 38% in 2008 as the Great Recession set in along with the financial crisis (people's 401k plans became 201k!); then the market rose by nearly 30% in 2013. This goes to demonstrate how volatile stocks can be; investors refer to this as "risk" – a reflection of *volatility* of stocks.

You may have noticed in this second diagram that the number of years during which the market rises exceeds the number of market declines – you are right. The stock market rises about two-third of the time and falls about one-third of the time. Over the longer term, on average, the stock market rises. The lesson in this is that you should not panic and sell your shares when the market falls, and especially not when the market declines sharply, as it did starting in January 2008 through mid-2009, unless we are in a serious and long-lasting crisis as in the 1930s.

Predictability of Stock Prices and Returns

The one thing that you should keep in mind is that stock prices and returns are very difficult to predict. Very few people, if any, have shown that they can forecast stock prices accurately enough and consistently, particularly in the short term – say, a week or a month in advance. But that hasn't stopped people over the years to attempt to predict or claim that they can foretell stock prices.

One approach that many stock forecasters have taken is the so-called *technical* analysis. It takes many forms. The analysts (who often refer to themselves as "technicians") typically use past or current data on stock prices and volumes to predict future stock prices. Here's a simple approach: if the price of a stock rises above its average price of the past 50 days, it signals a buy – that is, the price is likely to keep on rising. And if the price falls below the average, it signals a sell. (To be accurate, much more commonly, it is the "moving" average that technicians use). An enormous amount of research suggests that technical analysis fails, especially if one takes into account the transactions costs. In general, stock forecasters are generally quite vague about their forecasts, with lots of contingencies added to their predictions. For example, the technician may declare that stock prices may rise in the next six months and if prices don't fall below a certain level.

To explain why technical analysis may not work, let's consider a simple example. Suppose that you discover that over the last 10 years, stock X's price rises on the 3rd day of the month and then falls back on the 4th day of the month. What would you do? You buy it 2nd day of the month and sell it on the 3rd day. Easy money, right? Yes, if you are the only person who has discovered this about stock X. Pretty soon others will discover this property of stock X and will copy what you do. But when a lot of investors do this, as they all try to buy it on the 2nd day of the month, stock X's price will rise on that day, and when they all try to sell it on the 3rd day of the month, its price will fall. Consequently, stock X's price will now move in such a way to make it unlikely for you to earn the easy money that you thought you could: the opportunity is no longer there, and your system breaks down. Precisely this same situation occurred with small stocks during the months of December and January – the so-called *January effect*. It was discovered by some finance professors that small company stocks tended to fall in December and rise in January. As this pattern became widely known, investors took advantage of it and pretty soon there was no January effect.

Does this mean there is no technical system that works? No, it only means that once the pattern is widely disseminated, it will not work any longer. So, if you discover such a pattern keep it to yourself. Don't kill the goose that lays the golden egg.

Analysts also use another approach to help them predict stock returns; it is called *fundamental* analysis. This involves studying the company carefully, including its financial reports, its management and its plans, its competition and markets, the economy's condition, and so on. But there are other smart analysts and investors who are doing the same thing. To come out ahead of all the other investors, your outlook and prediction must be both <u>accurate</u> and <u>different</u> from those of the other investors. This is because if your outlook and prediction are the same as those of the other investors, even if accurate, you and they will buy or sell at the same time and the opportunity to earn abnormally high returns disappears.

It is useful to mention the reporters who discuss and, sometimes analyze, particular stocks or the market as a whole on financial TV channels. These reporters have no greater insight on stocks to offer than many investors and fund managers. Financial TV, like any other TV, including news, produces TV "shows". TV must be entertaining to attract viewers so that it can attract advertisers. Of course, these financial TV programs do provide some useful news and information. That's as far as they should be considered useful.

There are models developed over the years to decide whether the overall stock market is under- or overvalued at any particular time. This is different from forecasting individual stock prices. These overall market valuation models have been somewhat successful. For example, the price-earnings ratio (P/E) model can help determine whether the overall market is valued about right in terms of its past average performance. Given that the average P/E ratio has been around 15 for the past many decades (going back to the late 1800s), its current (August 2018) level of around 25 is quite high, suggesting that the market is perhaps overvalued. But the P/E ratio's "association" with market performance is not as strong as some other metric. There is a modified version of the P/E ratio model, called CAPE (Cyclically Adjusted P/E), developed by the Nobel Laureate Robert Shiller. It is available online. This version outperforms the simple P/E ratio. Using this measure, Shiller famously predicted the collapse of the market in late 1990. He is the person who first used the phrase "irrational exuberance".

One measure that seems to have a stronger relationship – that is, has a higher explanatory power – with market performance is the ratio of stocks to financial assets. Financial assets are the sum of stocks, bonds and cash in the economy. This metric was presented in *Philosophical Economics*, a publication that is available online, posted in December 2013. The plot of the measure is presented below. The logic of this measure is as follows. The <u>number</u> of shares remain relatively constant but their prices can change dramatically. The <u>values</u> of bonds and cash, however, remain relatively unchanged. If the ratio of the market value of stocks to financial assets is high, it must be that stock prices are too high. So according to this measure, the current level of the overall market appears to be too high and, therefore, the return on stocks in the future is likely to be low. It remains to see how well this index will perform in the future.

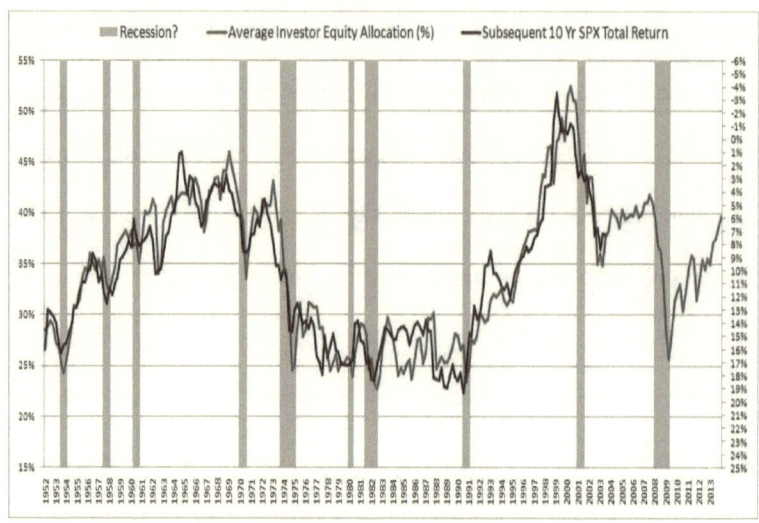

Source: Philosophical Economics

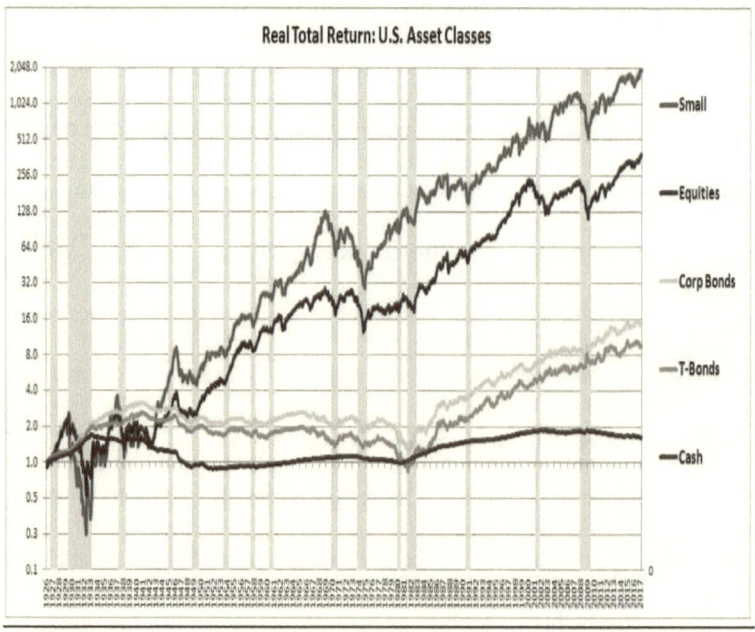

Some study *consumer sentiments* to determine the future path of stock prices. And there are investors who rely on stock price *momentum* to forecast stock prices. Consumer sentiments reflect how consumers view the economy and their own economic conditions; sentiments data are generally obtained through surveys. Momentum refers to the past price behavior of stocks. Recent research suggests that while consumer sentiments or stock price momentum do not individually help predict stock prices, a combination of the two does.

Stock Valuation

What determines the value of a stock? Since basically one invests in a business, a stock's value is based on how well the company is expected to do in the future. The generally accepted approach is to forecast the company's dividends, which itself is determined by the firm's profitability. How far into the future should one forecast the performance of the company? Since a company's life is theoretically infinite, then the appropriate horizon is infinite as well. Does this make sense?

Well, what if you forecast the firm's performance just for one year. Does that mean the you ignore what happens to the company beyond the one year? Clearly not, because next year's stock price has bearing on today's stock price. But what determines the stock price at the end of year 1 is based on the performance of the business in the subsequent year as well as its stock price at the end of year 2. Using similar logic, the price at the end of year 2 is determined by its stock price at the end of year 3. This means that this process has to repeated for many years into the future without any definite end time.

Thus, the dividends (or its *free cash flows*, which can be paid out as dividends) of a company for all future times must be forecast. To add these future dividends up we need to bring them to the present. In other words, we need to calculate the present values of these future cash flows and sum them up. This sum is the value of the company today; divide this figure by the number of shares outstanding and you arrive at the current share price.

The sticking point is that nobody can forecast a company's performance for an infinite number of future years; nobody can forecast them for even 20 years. Most analysts forecast company performance for the next 5 years, the ambitious analyst may go as far as 10 years. At the end of the forecast period one simply adds what is called *terminal value* to the sum of the present values of cash flows. Terminal value itself is determined on the basis of some simplifying assumptions, such as future cash flows growing at a constant rate for the indefinite future.

It should be clear by now why different analysts come up with different values for the same stock. First, one analyst's cash flow estimates may differ from another analyst's cash flow estimates. Second, they may use different time horizons to estimate future cash flows – one may use five years, another may use seven years, etc. Third, they may use different discount rates – one may use 12%, another may use 15%. And fourth, one analyst's terminal value may differ from another analyst's terminal value.

One other thing is involved and that is interest rates. When interest rates change so do discount rates that are used to compute cash flows. In addition, when interest rates rise, the economy weakens. This is because higher interest rates cause financing charges to increase on such things as credit card monthly charges, financing charges on car purchases, some mortgages, as well as financing charges businesses incur when they buy equipment and plant. These effects cause a reduction in business activity and therefore result in lower stock prices.

So now you are faced with more difficulty in stock investing. You must decide <u>which</u> stocks to buy and <u>when</u> to buy them.

Risk as a Factor Determining Stock Returns

Stocks are risky because the businesses they represent are risky. Sometimes these businesses do well, sometimes they even go bankrupt. It is this aspect of stocks that makes them risky.

Investment risk is measured by the volatility of returns of your investment; if returns didn't move up and down, the investment would not be risky. To be technical, one measures volatility by the *standard deviation* (which you may recall is the positive square root of variance) of the investment's return. Since you are showing such interest, you should know that the annual standard deviation of the average large company stock in the U.S. (i.e., the S&P500) is something like 20%. The riskier is an investment, the higher is its <u>expected</u> return. So high-risk stocks are expected to provide higher returns. And when the stock market as a whole becomes riskier – perhaps because there is greater uncertainty about the economy – the expected return on all stocks (the market itself) rises. Recall that the investor must be compensated for taking (market) risk and the higher is the risk, the higher is the expected compensation. One way this higher expected return is achieved is for current stock prices to decline; this occurs during economic downturns, when there is war, or when there is political uncertainty.

Price-Earnings Ratio

As a fast and ready measure, analysts and investors often use the Price-Earnings Ratio (P/E) of stocks to decide a stock's valuation. The inverse of P/E is Earnings per Share (EPS), which tells you the percentage return on the dollar amount you invest in the stock; for example, if the earnings is $2.50 per share and you pay $50 to acquire the stock, then your return is 5%. You can then compare this 5% with the 2.3% you receive on your savings or the return of 4.5% you would earn if you had invested in another stock. While useful as a first step, the use of P/E ratio is inadequate for several reasons. First, the riskiness of the stock that yields $2.50 per share may be quite different from another stock's; and in comparing returns on stocks with returns on bonds, the error may be substantial as many bonds are far less risky than stocks. And second, whether a stock is or is not a *growth* stock matters a lot.

But before going further, one issue needs to be discussed. There are two ways analysts measure EPS; one can use the current EPS. But EPS in one quarter may be abnormally high or low; to fix this problem analysts often use the *trailing 12-month* EPS, which is simply the average of the past twelve months' (actually the past four quarters) EPS. Sometimes the P/E ratio may seem too high, implying that the stock is too expensive. To improve the optics, analysts often use what they call *forward P/E* ratio; instead of past EPS, analysts use the one-year ahead forecast of EPS. The absurd thing about this is that forecasting earnings is not easy and subject to great uncertainty, so the forward P/E ratio should be viewed with a great deal of suspicion.

Growth stocks are stocks of companies whose earnings are growing very rapidly, by 15% per year or more, often significantly more. For a company's earnings to grow that fast, its sales must grow as fast or even faster. For example, Google's net income rose to $22.8 billion in 2017, an average increase of 17% since 2009, while its sales increased by an average of almost 21% per year to $111 billion during that period. Keep in mind that the US economy is expected to grow at something like 2% - 3% adjusted for inflation; adding to that another approximately 2% for inflation, the US economy's growth rate will be around 4% to 5%. Even if we include the entire world, we are talking about (optimistically) perhaps 5% to 6% per year. So, growing much faster than 6% or so for a long period becomes very difficult, even if we assume that no new competitors appear to grab market share. Be suspicious of ridiculously high stock prices that are said to be justified because of high expected growth rates.

One potential problem with growth stocks is that they are susceptible to sharp declines if their growth falls by even the slightest amount. On July 26, 2018 Facebook (FB) announced that its revenue is likely to grow more slowly during the second half of the year; the price of FB shares decline by nearly 20% within hours to $176. The market value of the company fell to $120 billion, with the CEO/Founder's wealth falling by some $15 billion as well. For perspective, market analysts had expected FB's revenues for the second quarter of 2018 to come in at $13.4 billion but revenues amounted to $13.2 billion, still an increase of 42% over the prior three months; profits increased as well, by 31% compared to the previous quarter. All of this happened because FB's daily active users were up by 11% as compared to 13% in the prior quarter. It should be added that FB had attracted political attention because of subscribers' personal data having been accessed by outsiders; but this issue had been around for months before the July 26 stock collapse; perhaps the data issue made the stock more susceptible to bad news.

Can you compare the P/Es of two companies to decide which has the less (or more) expensive stock? A qualified yes only if the two companies are about the same size and in the same industry. If one company is riskier than the other, everything else the same, the riskier company's stock should cost less and have a lower P/E ratio. When a company's profits are growing rapidly, investors are willing to pay more for its stock; P/E ratios of such companies tend to be higher as well. To adjust for growth rates, investors use the measure PEG, which is the P/E ratio divided by the growth rate of the company's earnings.

Consider Google (GOOG), General Motors (GM) and AT&T, Inc (T). Here are the measures of P/E for the three (given by a major brokerage firm):

Company	P/E (Trailing)	P/E (Forward)	PEG
GOOG	33.7	31.5	1.88
GM	8.9	6.14	0.62
T	17.3	9.0	2.78

While GOOG's forward P/E is nearly 5 times higher than GM's, its PEG is only 3 times higher, still high but not as high as the simple P/E; and while GOOG's P/E is nearly double the magnitude of T's, the latter's PEG is quite a bit higher than GOOG's. Presumably, T is overpriced even after correcting for its expected growth. Of course, what is missing is that these three firms are in three different businesses and thus not comparable.

Business Success and Stock Performance

Remember that a share of stock represents a share in a business – of selling cars or houses, importing and selling TV sets from Korea, importing shoes from China (did you know that some 90% of all shoes sold in U.S. are made in China?), running a for-profit hospital, selling clothes in department stores, and so on. If these businesses do well, then the shares in these businesses earn higher incomes and therefore rise in value; if a business is not doing well, its share values decline. A rapidly growing business is usually a sign that it is doing well – think of Starbuck's – and its share price rises.

When do businesses do well? In general, when the economy is growing businesses thrive. Therefore, you want to keep your eyes on the economy and government policy. But there are some businesses that do relatively poorly when the economy is doing well. For example, low-quality, cheap beer makers suffer during good times as people switch to better quality beer. And as people's earnings rise when the economy is strong, they shop less in discount stores and these businesses are not as profitable. Even when the economy is stagnant, a business that comes up with new products or services that are in greater demand will do well.

It is always necessary to know where the economy is going, up or down, expanding or contracting. But here's a secret: economists just don't have the right tools to forecast very accurately. It is extremely difficult to predict the turning points in the economy – the point when the economy starts a recovery or when it falls into a recession. There is a committee of prominent economists organized by the private organization the National Bureau of Economic Research (NBER) that decides the timing of these turning points – when the recession starts and when it ends – but this decision is made months <u>after</u> the fact. Therefore, it is an extremely difficult task to *time* the stock market. If you could time the market, you would sell just before the market turns down and buy just prior to market turns up; if you had this ability, instead of earning "puny" returns of 5%-7% per year, you would earn multiple of these returns, perhaps double or triple those rates. What difference does that make? A great deal. If you invest $100 at 7% per year for 20 years you end up with $387; at 14% you end up with $1,374, three and one-half times higher.

Outstanding Fund Managers and Forecasters

One often hears that a few investors and fund managers have a superior track in the sense that their investments have resulted in unusually high returns. Warren Buffett comes to mind as one such person. We'll return to Buffett shortly, but let's look at the general population of fund managers.

There are about 26,000 fund managers worldwide, of whom 20% (too few) are women. In the U.S., there are some 8,000 fund managers; only 10% of these are women (Germany also has relatively few female fund managers). Every year, some of them are crowned as "super" fund managers because of the extraordinary returns they deliver on their investment portfolios. Many investors look at the 5-year or 10-year track records of the funds individuals manage to decide with which funds they should invest their money.

Let's play a game of pure chance: start out with 8,000 (what statisticians call "fair") coins and flip them. If heads, call it a win and keep the coin; if tails, call it a fail and discard the coin. As you know, pure chance tells you that about one-half the coins will land heads and one-half will land tails. So, in the first round, you end up keeping approximately 4,000 coins (those that landed heads). Play the game another round and, following the same rule, now you end up with about 2,000 coins. If you play this game until you have one coin left, you end up with these coin numbers as winners (these are approximate figures, of course) : 8,000; 4,000; 2,000; 1,000; 500; 250; 125; 63; 32; 16; 8; 4; 2; 1. You don't know which of the coins you started out with ended up the winner – it was strictly by chance that this particular coin landed heads after all the flips. You have played the game 13 rounds and ended up with one winner. Of course, due to the randomness of coins coming up heads or tails, it is likely to end up with more than one winner by the 13th round or even with zero winners. You could have started playing this game 13 years ago, playing it only once a year to end up with one winning coin.

Note that if we take the 4,000 losers in round 1 and play the game with them, we may well end up with one who has won every toss for the last 12 years. Now we have another "star" coin. That one can find stars among the 4,000 losers is an insight Mehrdad Mehrain came up with.

Now take the 8,000 fund managers and study their returns over the years. After ten years, you are likely to find 8 of them doing superbly well. Should you invest your money with them? Are these managers any different from the mindless coins? After 13 years you have a superstar! He or she has outperformed all the other 8,000 fund managers; this person definitely deserves a multimillion-dollar reward, right? Don't conclude that these star investors are not superior, but also consider that pure chance alone could have resulted in this outcome. In other words, when someone beats the market even over many years, it is difficult to determine whether that person is lucky or has unusual skills. The same thing applies to fund managers: the few with outstanding performances could be due to just pure luck.

The average stock investment returns exactly the average overall stock market return because that is the meaning of average. If the return of the overall stock market is 6.4%, then if you take the return each stock investor has earned, add them up and divide by all the stocks, you end up with the overall market return. What this means is that if the returns on some stocks are higher than the return on the overall market, then returns on some other stocks must be lower. So if some stock portfolios earn returns that are higher than the overall market return, there must necessarily be other portfolios that earn less than the overall stock market return.

How about Mr. Buffett? His Berkshire Hathaway (BRK) umbrella investment company has done spectacularly well. In the past 11 years, it has earned 9% per year (Berkshire Hathaway has two classes of shares, A and B; here we discuss only the Class A shares). But even Warren Buffett's company took a beating between late January 2018 and early July 2018 – it lost some 13%. Some have said that what apparently has helped BRK at least in part is that it owns a major insurance company and the funds from that business have been used as leverage to enhance returns (we discussed *leverage* earlier; leverage magnifies your returns – benefiting you when you earn positive returns and killing you when you lose; it is like a lever!). Nevertheless, we cannot dismiss the possibility that Buffett and his business partner Charlie Munger have extraordinary stock acumen.

How to Ensure that You Invest in the "Right" Stocks

Since 1926 some 26,000 companies have listed their stocks on the three major U.S. stock exchanges. The vast majority of these stocks were subsequently delisted because of unprofitability, bankruptcies, mergers, being taken private, and so on. Altogether, they added about $35 trillion to the wealth of their shareholders. But only 5 stocks accounted for 10%, or nearly $3.5 trillion, of the $35 trillion gain; they are ExxonMobil, Apple, Microsoft, General Electric (GE), and International Business Machines

(IBM). Only about 1,100 of these companies generated the entire gain of $35 trillion. The other stocks just matched the one-month U.S. government one-month bonds (commonly known as Treasury bills), with better than one-half of these stocks delivering lifetime negative returns – that is, investors lost money on these stocks. In fact, individual stocks have a life of about 7-8 years before they disappear from an exchange.

The moral of these observations is that unless you are really exceptional in identifying great stocks, you are likely to miss them and end up investing in "dogs". To avoid that you want to invest in a large number of stocks shot-gun style, so you construct a *diversified portfolio*; sure, you will have dogs in your investment portfolio, but you will also invest in the great ones: these days it appears that Amazon, Apple, Google, Facebook, and Netflix might be among the great ones. I should add that it seems that GE has now joined the "dogs" group as it had dropped to around $8 by December 2018, from a high of $33 in November 2016. This too illustrates how in a short period a great stock creates a huge loss for shareholders; had you invested in GE stock in 2016, you would have lost 76% of your money in that stock. Note that while going from $33 to $8 involves a loss of 76%, but to go from $13 back to the $33 price involves a rise of better than 313%, a herculean effort.

Mechanics of Investing in Securities

You decide to use some of your savings to invest in securities. The question is what rules you should follow. Your stock broker may periodically inform you of specific stocks to buy. She may tell you that stock XYZ priced at $73 per share is a good buy. Since it is customary to buy stock in lots of 100 shares, this may mean that you will spend $7,300 on this recommendation. When will the next recommendation arrive? Perhaps in two months and that may require an investment of $3,200. Alternatively, you may send your broker $520 every three months to invest for you as she sees fit. Some of the money may be invested in stocks, some in government bonds and some in corporate bonds.

There are various rules one can follow. One method is to invest a fixed amount of money in stocks every month. This is called *dollar-cost averaging*: buy a fixed dollar amount of stocks every month. Using this rule, you spend the same amount of money, say $250, every month but buy fewer shares when prices are high and buy more shares when prices are low.

The Nobel Laureate Daniel Kahneman said that in investing, you should follow a policy to minimize your future *regret*. Incidentally, psychologists and neuroscientists have determined that humans are more averse to regret than they relish success. One way to avoid this state of affairs is to not get too exuberant when the market is way up nor get petrified when the market falls sharply, as it did during the Great Recession of 2008. The S&P 500 hit a low of 683 on March 5, 2009 but closed at 2827 on August 21, 2018, more than quadrupling in a little more than 9 years. This is about an average increase of about 16% per year; given that there was little inflation during this period, the real (inflation adjusted) return in stocks of this magnitude is phenomenal. Had you sold while the market was falling like a rock during the 2008-2009 period, you would have lost this tremendous opportunity to make tons of money.

Buying on Margin, Selling Short

Suppose you have $1,000 in your bank and you think that the stock of GE is likely to rise from a price of $13.75 to $17.50 in a few months. You want to buy 100 shares of GE, which will cost you $1,375, plus a few dollars in commissions and fees (these days, these amount to no more than around $10). You can borrow the $375, but from whom? Well, your broker would gladly lend you the difference but of course for a price – at the interest rate of around 4% these days. The stock that you buy for $1,375 now becomes the collateral for the loan; this is called buying stock on *margin*. Note that a margin transaction is simply leverage.

Let the GE stock reach $17.50 and according to your plan you close your position (i.e., sell your shares); you pay back the $375 loan plus the interest you owe to your broker. The reason you sell your stock is that you think that GE stock is on a downward trajectory for the next few months. After the experience of doing so well on the prior transaction, now you want to go big time. How do take advantage of this insight? Well, you can sell GE stock now that its price is "high" according to you. But you don't own any GE shares. Here's how you can do it: Borrow 300 shares of GE from someone who owns them and promise to give them back to her in the future. But do you know anyone with 300 shares of GE who is willing to lend them to you? Probably not. But your friendly broker is always ready to help. Call him and tell him your intentions; he'll find exactly what you need. He'll borrow the GE shares and sell them for you; this is called selling a security *short* or *shorting* a security – selling a security you don't own. The broker doesn't have to look for a stockholder. Nowadays when you buy stock, you don't usually take possession of the shares; the shares are held for you by the broker in the *street name* and the broker uses these to short sell for you. He'll keep the proceeds from the sale himself as collateral for the loan. When the stock falls in value you can buy the shares at a price lower than when you borrowed them, keep the profit, and the broker gives the shares back to the investor from who they were borrowed.

In the above examples the assumption was that things turned out as you expected them. Alas, the real world doesn't always work in our favor. What if the stock price rises? If the price rises sufficiently, the amount of money the broker has kept is no longer sufficient to cover your loss and you are required to deposit more funds or else your position would be liquidated. If, even after your position is "closed" (that is, liquidated) the funds are insufficient, you are liable and must make up the difference.

Day Trading

Starting 2-3 decades ago some people became active in what is called *day trading*. Day trading generally involves buying and selling securities on the same day. By the late 1990s there were some 4,000-5,000 active day traders in the U.S. Their activity now accounts for about one-seventh of the volume on the Nasdaq. These are people who have quit their jobs and businesses and have devoted their time to day trading. Day trading participation is correlated with the performance of the stock market. More investors get into the day trading act when the stock market is on an upswing. Similarly, more people get into real estate sales when the housing market is hot. In 2000-2002 when the stock market was doing poorly, day trading was squelched. One reason may be that when the market is rising, one can buy when during the day the market is weaker and sell when it rebounds.

Academicians have conducted studies to determine whether day trading is profitable. While not definitive, the overall conclusion is that once the transactions costs are taken into account, day trading is not profitable. These costs include payments for the use of software and hardware, rent for a place in the office of the trading company, commissions and taxes (remember that these profits are taxed as short-term gains which are higher than long-term capital gain). A study of day traders in Taiwan concluded that while the average day trader did not make a profit, those who traded heavily (i.e., those committing larger sums of money) and had a strong past performance did earn very high profits.

In this connection it is worthwhile to mention that <u>frequent</u> traders do not come ahead. Interestingly, a study concluded that female investors tended to trade less frequently than male investors and that the female investors earned higher returns than their male counterparts.

Chapter 12

BONDS

Your friend is short $200 to buy a used motorcycle for $450 but he expects to receive a $600 tax refund in two weeks. He asks you for a loan of $200 for two weeks and promises to repay you the $200 plus a bonus of $3, just because you are nice; you agree. You may not know it, but your friend has just created a *bond*. Any time there is borrowing and lending a bond is created – that's all there is to a bond, regardless of who is involved in the transaction.

Note the following about this bond that was just created. First, there is the sum that your friend promises to pay back the money she borrows, the $200; this is called the *principal* or *face value* or *par value* of the bond. Second, she promises to pay you something extra on top of the principal, the $3; this is called *interest*. Third, she also promises to make the payment in two weeks; this is called *maturity*, in this case two weeks. Fourth, notice that all the payments are *promised* payments. She could take your money, buy the bike and ride to who knows where and you'd never see her or your money again. Finally, you have made the loan strictly on the basis of her word; if she decides to not repay the loan you have essentially no recourse other than legal action. Even if you take her to court and get a judgment against her, she could declare bankruptcy; she will walk away and owe you nothing, especially if she owns nothing (she may have sold the bike and spent the money). In your case, you have extended a loan without a *collateral*. A collateral is something that belongs to you (at least partially) if the borrower *defaults* on the loan – that is, if she fails to make the promised interest or principal payments.

When you buy a car on credit, you sign a contract. Usually, you make a down payment; the difference between the price of the car and your down payment is the amount of the loan, the principal. The contract is the bond. It is a "hard-copy" bond, as opposed to the loan you made to your friend to buy a motorcycle which was a "verbal" bond. The car bond specifies the *size* of your periodic payments as well as their *timing*. If you make payments for five years, then the bond's maturity is five years. Notice that such bonds usually involve monthly fixed payments – that is, the size of your monthly payments does not change, staying at $326 per month, for instance. This is an amortizing bond that we saw earlier in the case of a mortgage so each payment consists of interest and partial repayment of the principal. Again, as discussed before, the earlier payments include mostly interest and little principal and the later payments cover little interest and mostly principal.

As before, the repayment of the loan and interest is based on your word, your promise. But the difference between your car purchase and the loan you made to your friend for her bike is that in this case the contract with the car dealer stipulates that if you fail making the payments the dealer will repossess the car (there are folks who earn their living doing just that:

repossessing cars for the lender, and yes, they are tough and often carry guns). This loan is *collateralized*, the car being the collateral. The collateral provides a little more guarantee for the lender that he will recover his funds, both because the borrower has a stronger incentive to pay off the loan and because by repossessing the car and selling it the lender recovers the loan (often this alternative involves partial recovery of the loan).

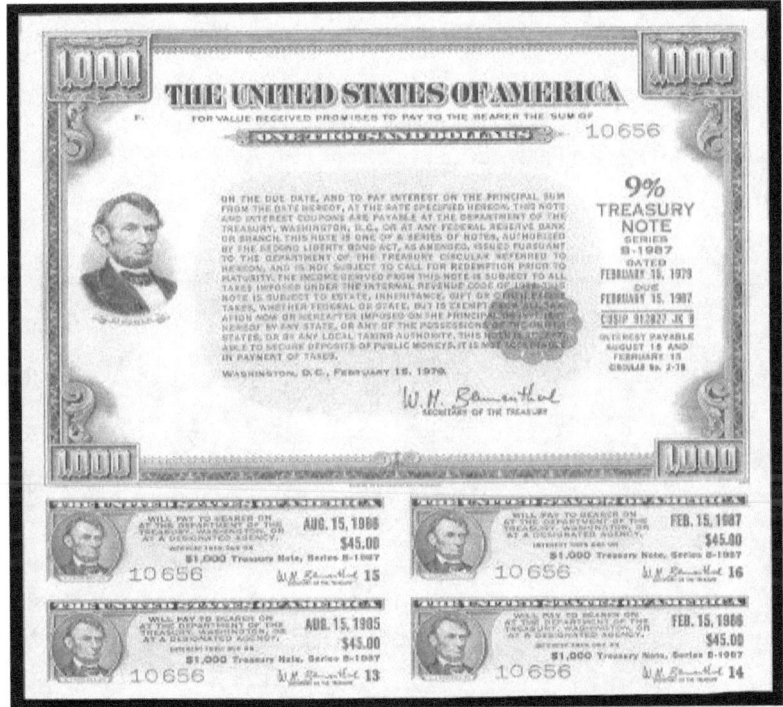

US Treasury Coupon Note with
Detachable 6-month Interest Coupons (only 4 coupons shown)

As you know by now, loans are made for various lengths of time – a multitude of maturities. Professionals have given various names to bonds of different maturities. Bonds that mature within one year are called *bills*. Between one-year and ten-year maturities, bonds are referred to as *notes*. Bonds with maturities longer than ten years are referred to as *bonds*. Although, these terms are often reserved for U.S. government bonds, people may use them to refer to private sector bonds as well. Often bills, particularly U.S. government bills, are sold at a discount from the principal value. For example, if the issuer promises to pay you $1,000 in one year, the bill is sold to you for $996.00; you get paid $1,000 when the bill matures which means that you have earned an interest of $4.0 or a <u>rate</u> of return of 4.02% (the 0.02% extra because you invested $996, not $1,000).

US Treasury 6-Month $100,000 (Discount) Bill.

Notice that Interest is Not Specified

Now what is a *CD*? CD is the abbreviation of Certificate of Deposit and it is a bond as well. A financial institution, usually a bank, sells these to the public. You buy a one-year CD for $1,000 from your friendly neighborhood bank and the bank promises to pay you back your $1,000 plus 2.50% interest if you leave your funds with the bank for the full one year. This means that you lend your bank $1,000, the principal, and earn $2.50, the interest, if you leave your money at the bank for one year, the CD's maturity. The bank's payments are also promises; often the government guarantees these funds, at least up to a certain amount (in the hundreds of thousands of dollars). But even here it is still the promise of the government that provides the security of the CD. There is no collateral. Speaking of collateral: many corporate bonds are issued without collateral and are called *debentures*; debentures are *unsecured*.

Now that you have learned all these terms, let's be a bit more complete. The face value is what the issuer promises to pay you when the bond matures, after the final interest is paid. Someone borrows $100 from you to buy a chair, promises to pay you $2.40 every six months for 24 months and return your $100 at the same time that the fourth interest is paid. In the real world, interest on bonds is usually paid every six months. Being a cautious person, you get this agreement in the form of an official contract, with witnesses and signatures, the whole shebang. The interest on this bond is $2.40 every six months, for annual rate of 4.80% (actually it can be a little more than 4.8% since you can reinvest the $2.40 you received after six months and earn interest on it as well) and a face value of $100. Unless she has a contract that specifies that you can take the chair in case she fails to pay either interest or the principal, this is a debenture.

Liquidity of Bonds and Price Effect

As discussed earlier, some assets are easy to sell at their true market prices; these we called liquid assets (cash is the most liquid of assets, with US government bills close behind). Some assets are not easy to sell at their fundamental market prices; these are illiquid assets and include real estate, jewelry, and used furniture. It takes a relatively long time to receive near-market prices for illiquid assets.

Many bonds are quite illiquid. Municipal bonds in particular are illiquid in the sense that the *bid-ask* spread for them is quite high (*bid* is the price a broker is ready to buy and *ask* is the price he is willing to sell). You may pay 105% of the true market value of the bond when you buy it, and if you try to sell it soon after you may get only 95% of its market value. This is because the dealer of the bond may have to hold it for an extended period before he can find a buyer for it. During that time, interest rates can change significantly or the issuer's financial condition may deteriorate. This problem is ubiquitous with some sovereign bonds as well, especially during times when the issuer is experiencing financial or economic uncertainty. In contrast, bonds issued by the U.S. Treasury and the governments of Germany, Switzerland, and Japan are among the most liquid of assets.

Attributes of Bonds

Consider the example of a bond that pays $50 per year for 4 years and also pays the $1000 amount borrowed in that fourth year (so the payment in year 4 is $1050). The $50 payment is the *interest* plus the *principal* (the $1,000 here). The sum of the present value of these cash flows, if the discount rate is 6% is $965.35. So, if you are out there trying to buy this bond, that is precisely how you would determine how much the bond is worth. In the real world, bonds are traded in a market so their prices are given to you; the market has made the calculation.

As we have seen a bond specifies the maturity of the bond, the principal, and the interest payments. These attributes are not subject to change – they are fixed. The only thing that can change is the discount rate, 6% in our example. The discount rate changes when all interest rates in the economy change, or if the riskiness of this particular bond changes. If the discount rate for bonds similar to the one we have here has risen to 7%, then the discount rate on this bond will rise to 7% as well. Therefore, the discounted value of the future cash flows on this bond must be adjusted as well, as shown below

$$\$932.26 = \frac{1}{(1+0.07)^1} \times 50 + \frac{1}{(1+0.07)^2} \times 50 + \frac{1}{(1+0.07)^3} \times 50$$
$$+ \frac{1}{(1+0.07)^4} \times 1050$$

$$= 46.73 + 43.67 + 40.81 + 801.04$$

Because the discount rate is higher the price of the bond falls, to $932.26 versus $965.35 before. Of course, this is due to the fact that every discounted cash flow is now lower than before. Now try a discount rate of 4%. You get $1,036.30. The conclusion is that as the discount rate changes, the price of the bond changes in the "opposite" direction. Here's an interesting exercise: what is the price of this bond if its discount rate were 5%; you have probably noticed that the periodic interest payments of $50 amounts to 5% of the principal. Well, it turns out that the price of this bond with 5% discount rate is exactly $1,000, the value of the principal. Whenever you have the interest on a bond as percentage of its principal the same as its discount rate, the price of the bond (the present value of its cash flows) is exactly equal to its principal. Try interest of $50 and principal of $900 with a discount rate of 5.556% – you should get $900.

When a company wants to borrow – that is, issue a bond – it tries to set the interest payment as close to the discount rate on the bond as possible so that it can sell the bond for the principal of the bond, so that it can borrow the principal value of the bond. Once issued, of course, the price of the bond can change only if the discount rate changes (e.g., due to a change in interest rates throughout the economy or because of a change in the riskiness of the bond).

Let's spend a moment to clarify confusing terminology. In the bonds market, "interest rates" and "discount rates" are often used interchangeably. However, *interest* applies only to what we have used in discussing our example, the $50 periodic payments. But when investors talk about interest rates, they generally have in mind the discount rate, our 6% or 7% or 4%. Since bond prices and interest rates (remember, these are the discount rates 6%, 7% or 4%) move in opposite directions, market participants tend to focus on "rates", as opposed to bond "prices". When they say "rates have risen" the implication is that bond prices have fallen. This must be so since the periodic payment, principal and maturity of a bond are fixed, so the only thing that can change the bond price is its discount rate.

Examples used above use interest payments made once a year; however, bonds in general pay their periodic interests every six months, not annually. But that is a mere detail that can be handled easily. In our example, instead of $50 each year the bond will pay $25 every six months, so there will be 8 discounting period over the four years that it takes for the bond to mature. You would then use one-half the discount rate (divide it by 2) and raise the exponents by one-half of what we have here as well. Thus, the discount rate for the 6% case becomes 3% and the exponents become ½, 1, 1½, 2, 2½, 3, 3½, 4.

Back to the example of lending your friend $200 and let's say that you have a paper signed by your friend attesting that she owes you $200 and will pay you back $215 in one year; this is a bond. Your bank offers to buy this bond from you for $207 but you decline the offer. Suppose that a couple of days later someone contacts you and wants to sell a watch for $240. Being very smart, you know that this is a good enough watch to be worth $270; but sadly enough you have only $180. The only way can get your hands on more cash is to somehow cash out the money you lent to your friend. Unfortunately for you, the Fed has raised the interest rates it can control directly and as a result all interest rates in the country have increased; in fact, you now regret that you lent the $200 at a rate of interest that seems too low in retrospect. Lucky for you it happens that there is a market for bonds that have been issued in the past. You take your bond to the market trying to sell it. The best offer you receive is $190. Why? Because as interest rates across the board have risen so have the discount rates, including the discount rate on your bond. As shown above, when the discount rate increases, the price of bonds fall.

Bonds may seem boring investments. But they are not. You now know that as interest (discount) rates change so do bond prices. If interest rates are volatile, bond prices will be too. There is a whole industry whose job is to forecast interest rates and, therefore, bond prices. Several measures have been developed to help understanding and forecasting bond prices. One such measure is *convexity*; convexity relates the price of a bond to its discount rate. What is involved is that when interest rates are low, bond prices are very high, and a small change in interest rates results in a very large change in bond prices. In contrast when interest rates are high, bond prices are low and even a big change in interest rates cause a relatively small change in bond prices. This is shown in the figure below.

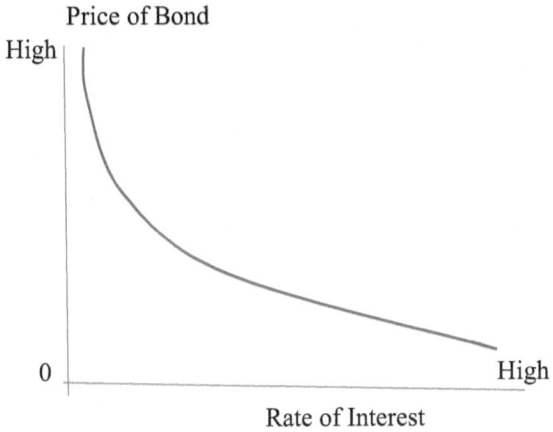

Different Types of Bonds

In our discussion so far we have assumed that bonds mature at some point in the future. But there exist bonds that never mature; they just keep paying their interest. In England these bonds are referred to as *consols*. There exist some bonds, and they are quite popular, that pay no interest at all, called *zero-coupon* bonds or simply *zeros*; the bondholder just gets the principal value of the bond at maturity. When you buy a zero-coupon bond, you pay less than the principal (face value) of the bond; at maturity you get paid the full value; the difference in purchase price and face value is your return. Some U.S. government bonds, the ones with maturities of one year or less (recall these are Treasury "bills") are zero-coupon bonds.

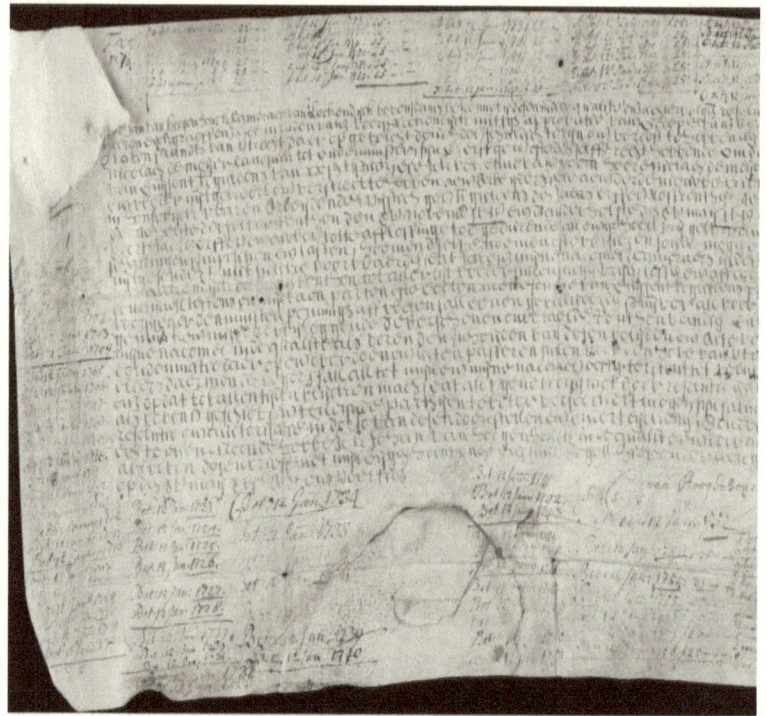

This perpetual bond issued by the Dutch water authority in 1648 continues to pay, yielding around €11.65 a year. (PHOTO: YALE UNIVERSITY)

In the past several decades, inflation has run at an average of around 3% per year. This means that if you had $100 in cash, this cash lost 3% of its value or purchasing power each year. So, if you owned a bond with the face value of $1,000 that matured in two years, you would get the face value at maturity but your $1,000 would have only about $940 in today's purchasing power. This tends to make some bonds less attractive to some investors – e.g., to someone who buys a bond hoping to retire in 10 years on the cash the bond brings at maturity, but the face value of this bond would have about one-third less buying power in 10 years. To alleviate this problem, some issuers have devised way to adjust for inflation. One such bond is the U.S. Treasury Inflation Protected Securities, or TIPS for short. TIPS adjust the face value of the bond once a year based on the inflation rate experienced in the prior year. For example, if the face value is $1,000 and inflation in the preceding year was 2.5%, then the face value is adjusted up to $1,025. Since the interest paid on a bond is expressed in percentage terms (e.g., as 4.0% per year), then the interest payment itself is also adjusted up to account for inflation. To illustrate, the first year interest on the bond is $40.00; if inflation the next year amounts to 2.5%, then the interest in the second year rises to $41.00, still 2.5% of the new principal.

Another interesting class of bonds is *convertible* bonds. A convertible bond, as its name suggests, converts to a common share at some point in the future at a given conversion ratio – for example, each bond converts to four shares starting in eight years. These bonds are a composite of an ordinary bond and a call option (options are discussed in Chapter 16).

Then there is a class of bonds referred to as *callable* bonds. With these bonds the issuing company has the right to have the holder of the bond turn in her bond in return for some cash. Such bonds specify the time at which they may be called and the price at which they will be repurchased. Many bonds issued by companies are callable despite their stated maturity.

The final class of important bonds discussed here are the *municipal* bonds or *munis*. Munis are bonds issued by municipalities or states. Their main distinguishing feature is that their returns are exempt from federal income taxes; this feature is the result of the historical sovereignty of states. In addition, if the owner of a muni is a resident of the issuing state, the returns are free of the state income taxes as well. The tax exemption feature means that the investor is happy with a lower return; consequently, munis carry lower interest rates than other bonds. It should be noted that just as munis are exempt from federal taxes, interest on U.S. Treasury bonds are exempt from state and local taxes as well (but not exempt from federal taxes).

It turns out that the expression we have presented here for determining bond values is useful for understanding the value of stocks as well. There are three differences, however. One is that instead of interest, stocks pay dividends and dividends can and do vary. Second, in principle, the life of a company is infinite or at least very long (e.g., GE has been around for over 100 years) but bonds have limited maturities (with the exception of very limited number of bonds). Third, companies usually pay dividends every three months, instead of every six months for bonds. But it should be noted that when interest rates change across the board, the discount rates used for stocks tend to change as well, just as they do for bonds.

Treasury Bills Return and Inflation

Due to their importance this section covers US Government bills. The return on one-year Treasury bills (T-bills) averaged 4.92% per year during the 39 years 1978-2017; during that same period, inflation as measured by the Consumer Price Index for urban residents averaged a little more than 3.45%. So, this security has beaten inflation by 1.47% per year. How nice! At this rate of 1.47% an investment of $100 in 1978 would double in 47 years; contrast this with 7% which doubles the value of your investment in ten years or 3.5% which doubles it in 20 years. The situation has been even worse in the past ten years: over the period 2008-2017, your investment in T-bills would have grown by an average of 0.4% per year while inflation would have eaten into your purchasing power by 1.7% per year.

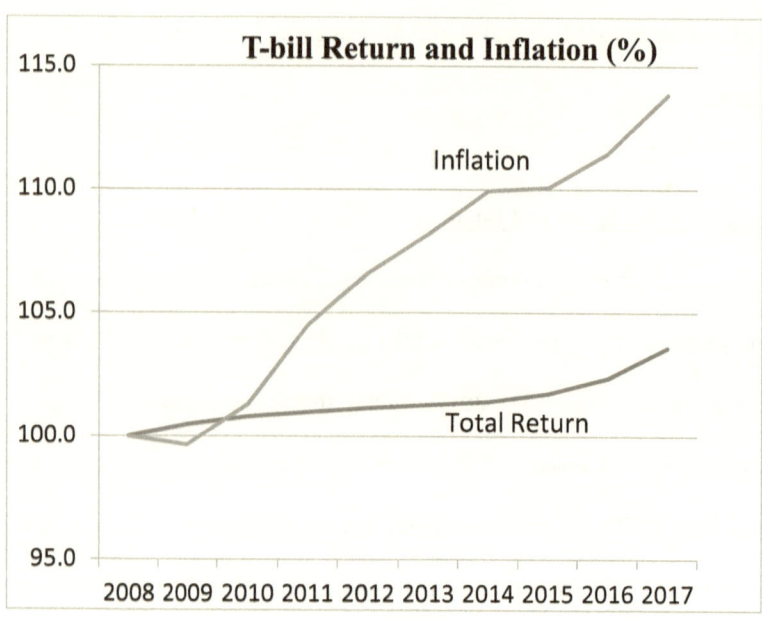

The above figure depicts the <u>accumulated</u> return on U.S. Treasury bills during the ten years 2008-2017 versus inflation. If you had $100 invested in T-bills in 2008 you would have accumulated a total of $103.60 by 2017. On the other hand, to maintain the purchasing power of your $100, you would have needed $113.80 by 2017. In other words, to keep your purchasing power intact you would have needed an extra $13.80 by 2017; but T-bills would have provided you with only an extra $3.60, a shortfall of about $10. Granted that these ten years were particularly bad for Treasury securities due to the Great Recession, but when one invests one has to take the bad with the good.

It bears repeating that T-bills are as free of risk as nearly any security or asset one can think of and, accordingly, if one wants to avoid risk then investment in T-bills is justified. Furthermore, even if T-bills do not cover the erosion of your funds due to inflation, they do cover it at least in part, which is better than cash. In the above figure, sitting on cash you would lose $13.80 but the T-bills investment would cover $3.60 of that.

Connection Between Long Term and Short Term Interest Rates

There is a connection between short term and long term interest rates. It turns out that long term rates are some sort of the average of <u>current</u> and <u>future</u> short term rates; therefore, long term rates can indicate the level short term rates are likely to be in the future.

Here is an example to demonstrate the relationship between short- and long-term interest rates. You have $100 extra to save for two years. Your bank tells you that you can deposit the funds in an account that pays 7% per year compounded as long as you do not withdraw the principal or the interest for the two-year period. Since the interest is compounded, at the end of the two years you have $100(1.07)^2 = 114.49. The bank also offers you the alternative to pay you 5% the first year and promises 8% the second year if you reinvest the accumulated funds in the second year; under this alternative you end up with $100(1.05)(1.08) = 113.40. Obviously, you will choose the first alternative, as will all potential depositors. What happens next is that the bank realizes that it is offering a better deal with the 7% for two years than with the 5% and 8% alternative in each year separately. The bank will either lower the two-year rate of 7% or raise the

5%-8% combination, or both. This adjustment will go on until depositors like you become indifferent between the two alternatives.

We have names for the 7%, 5% and 8% rates. The 7% and 5% rates are called *spot* rates; the 8% rate is called the *forward* rate. Any interest rate that is effective as of today is a spot rate. Any rate that is agreed to be paid on funds lent in the future is a forward rate. If you are buying a house and find a bank to lend you the mortgage at 4.5% upon closing in two months, this 4.5% is a forward rate because the act of lending to you the mortgage takes place in the future. Spot and forward (and futures) are discussed in more detail in Chapter 16.

Yield Inversion

If we plot short-term and long-term spot rates of interest against their maturities we have what's called the *yield curve*; it is customary to focus on the U.S. Treasury securities yield curve. In normal times the yield curve is upward sloping – i.e., it rises as maturity increases, as shown below.

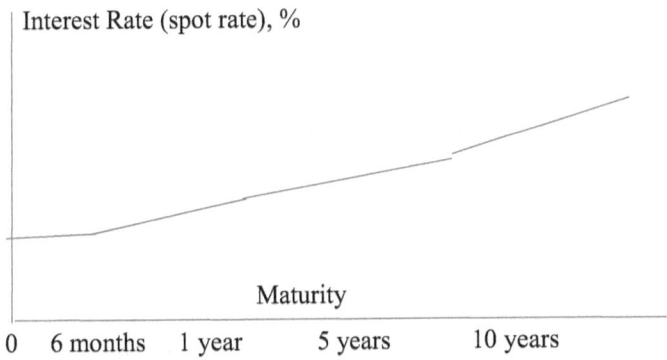

Sometimes the yield curve becomes flat and occasionally it slopes downward so that short term rates exceed long term rates; this is referred to as an *inverted yield curve*. Investors pay a great deal of attention to the shape of the yield curve because in the past inverted yield curves have predicted a recession in the near future. Recent research suggests that the best yield predictor of a recession is the gap between the three-month and ten-year U.S. Treasury securities. The New York Fed uses the Treasury yield curve to come up with the likelihood of recessions and it has a decent record of being correct. There are some, including some at the Fed, who argue that yield curve inversion no longer predicts recessions. Well, that remains to be seen. It is best to act to protect yourself in case these economists are mistaken in their views.

Chapter 13

COLLECTIBLES, ART WORK, AND ANTIQUES

You can spend a lot of money on *collectibles*. Collectibles can be anything: stamps, baseball cards, magazines, toys, old empty boxes, advertising prints, old beer cans, old wheel hubcaps, on and on. You must be passionate about what you collect because some of this stuff has no value to other people. If of no value to others you cannot make money on them. Your reward is having them, period. Some collectibles such as stamps and baseball cards enjoy a large market and can be very valuable. But collectibles that command high prices today may lose their value in the future because for a variety of reasons; usually it is because people may lose interest in them. The sport card of a famous hockey player lost much of its worth after the player was injured and stopped playing.

Sport Card and 1960 U.S. Air Mail Stamp

Antiques too can lose their worth because of change in tastes and interests. Here's my take on much of antiques: 100-200 years ago the garbage collection system was poor or nonexistent so a lot of what we now consider antique is just inherited junk. What is so attractive about a 150-year old chair with one broken leg and worn out seat cover priced at $18,000? Furthermore, if you fix the leg and repair the seat cover, the chair loses one-half of its value.

No Difference Between Antiques and Junk
(from the TV show Sanford and Son)

Interestingly, some antiques that were not worth that much just a couple of decades ago have become highly valuable all of a sudden. This happened to Chinese antiques and art work as China became wealthier and the Chinese desired to own items that represented Chinese heritage.

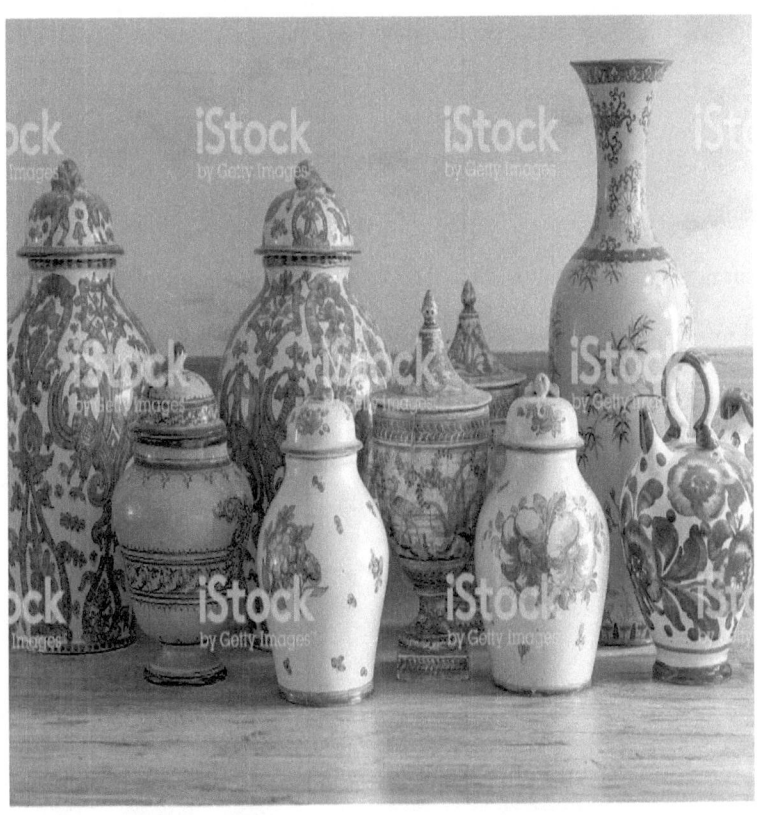

Antique Chinese Pottery

Of course, the granddaddy of them all are *art work*: paintings and statues and other items considered pieces of art. To a large extent, it is the "who" that matters more than, a lot more than, the quality of the work. Among the most popular are the works of van Gough, Picasso and Gauguin but the style would probably be well-liked even if they were done by Joe Six-Pack. As proof of this assertion observe how some people paid millions of dollars to own a painting by Jason Pollock but when it was discovered that it was a fake, its value fell to a mere few hundreds of dollars. The

Hungarian Elmy de Hory painted some 1,000 fakes, similar to the paintings of highly sought-after artists including Modigliani, Degas, Matisse, and Picasso. It is said that perhaps as many as one-half of all paintings by famous artists are fake. But some fakes are quite good, selling for tens of thousands of dollars. While a real (at least thought to be real) painting can sell for $20-million, the known *fake* version can be worth "only" $15,000 – so good art is valuable, but only a small fraction of the same art done by a popular artist: marketing matters a lot (see below for another example).

Amedeo Modigliani, Nude Sitting on a Divan, 1917

Nowadays 3-D printers can reproduce works of arts that are impossible to distinguish from the original, except through the chemical and x-ray analyses of the paint and the canvas used. It is through such analyses that fakes are identified. In other words, it is not the quality of the original art compared to copies that determines value, but the original signature and the name of the artist herself or himself that determines what people are willing to pay for pieces of art. Another example of this is the prints of originals that are numbered and signed by the artist herself or himself, thus commanding prices sometimes in the thousands of dollars. It is true that the signature indicates that the artist has approved the quality of the print, but the same quality is easily obtainable; yet without the signature the print can sell for not much more than $20-$100. Another aspect of signed prints is to keep the number of prints small, otherwise the price of the prints would be low, exemplified by Chagall's work. He generated so many signed prints that their prices are quite low. It is the same law of demand and supply: keep supply down to achieve a higher price.

As I was completing this manuscript it was announced that a computer-made painting, using a computer code and without the help of a person, was sold for over $400,000. So perhaps the "art" itself was considered valuable by the buyer or was the high price reflected the value of novelty? But note that this computer code can potentially produce hundreds of such paintings per week (per day?) and other codes can be written to create even nicer paintings. With supply so abundant, one can imagine the price of computer-generated "art" to fall to near zero. Will we then be back with human art becoming even more valuable?

In acquiring collectibles and pieces of art for investment purposes you must forecast what will be popular or in great demand in the future. Which artist will be trendy? What will people want to be collecting? If you watch the TV program "Antique Roadshow" you probably have noticed that sometimes the show gives the price estimate of ten years ago and then offers the current price estimate, and often the current price is less than the older price.

Many expensive collectibles, especially art work, are sold at auctions conducted by auction houses. The auctioneer charges a commission, usually specified as a percentage of the selling price. Often the seller specifies a minimum price, called *reservation* price, below which the seller will not sell. It has become more common for the auctioneer to guarantee a minimum price on the item to be auctioned; if the auction price does not rise above the guaranteed price, the auctioneer pays the owner the guaranteed price. This guarantee is equivalent to a "put option" (please see Chapter 16 on options).

It has been observed that in some business auctions, such as oil companies bidding on new tracts to explore for oil, the bidding winner ends up losing on the project or earn less profit than the bidder expected. This is called the *winner's curse*. As the number of bidders increases, the bidding becomes more aggressive, pushing the price higher which, in turn, makes the winner less well off.

Chapter 14

PRECIOUS METALS AND CRYPTOCURRENCIES

<u>Precious Metals</u>

Precious metals are basically gold and silver and some may add platinum to the group. They come in the form of bullion and, for gold and silver, in the form of coins as well. When it comes to coins we exclude rare or old coins because their value is more related to their rarity than their content of precious metals. A rare silver Roman coin weighing one-quarter of an ounce may be worth $50,000 while its silver content is worth only $4 or less.

The first thing to note about precious metals, which they have in common with collectibles, is that they do not pay any interest or dividends. The second thing to note is that it is not easy to store them safely; they are subject to theft (e.g., burglary) or loss. You often incur a cost in storing them, as in a bank safety deposit box. Alternatively, you can buy them as jewelry to carry them on yourself most of the time, as in a ring, necklace or bracelet; of course, the jewelry cost more than the value of the gold or silver content.

Pure (99.99%) Gold and Silver 1 kg Bars

So why do people buy precious metals? Often people invest in precious metals as a protection against inflation. Zimbabwe established a new currency in 1980, calling it the Zimbabwe Dollar (ZWD) with ZWD 1.0 = US $1.0. The country experienced what's called *hyperinflation*, in the thousands of per cent per year – e.g., 66,000% per year in 2007 – so that ZWD 1.0 was hardly worth 1 US cent after a few years. Zimbabwe redenominated its currency several times, calling them the second dollar, the third dollar, and so on. By the time it suspended its currency altogether in 2009, one US cent could buy ZWD 100 trillion; Zimbabweans could then use any currency they wished in transactions. In such a situation Zimbabweans might buy gold instead of keeping their savings in their own currency. Of course, they could also accumulate reliable currencies such as the US dollar, the British pound sterling, or the euro, if these currencies are available; if not available, the alternative would be precious metals.

The Zimbabwe currency worth around US$ 1 cent

The case of Zimbabwe is rare but not unique. After WWII, the Hungarian government had to print 100-quintillion notes (one quintillion is 1 followed by 18 zeros), the highest denomination ever produced. At the Hungarian inflation rate prices doubled in less than a day. Inflation in Venezuela started rising rapidly. In October 2017, the International Monetary Fund (IMF) forecast the rate of inflation in Venezuela to reach 2,300% in 2018. The IMF revised its forecast upward to 13,000% in January 2018. By July 2018, the IMF raised its forecast again, to an incredible 1,000,000 per cent. In late August 2018, the government devalued the bolivar from an exchange rate of 285,000 bolivar per US dollar to 6 million to $1. In situations like that nobody wants to hold on to paper money. Instead one wants to possess anything of any value. In the hyperinflationary period 1921-1924 in Germany, restaurant patrons paid when they placed their orders because by the time their food arrived its price had gone up.

Like pretty much everything else, the prices of precious metals are determined by both demand and supply. Precious metals have industrial use as well. Platinum is used extensively on auto emission control equipment; because of its conductivity silver is used in electronics; gold too is used in electronics, but also in dentistry and in various alloys. When price rises, supply increases because miners find it more profitable to extract more of the metal; and owners of the metal in various forms (jewelry, coins, etc.) also sell their holdings, adding to the supply. As price rises, the increase in price is checked further because users of the metals try to economize on their use.

Nowadays, with fairly easy access to foreign currencies and foreign securities, it is hard to justify precious metals as hedge against inflation, unless the inflation is worldwide. One can instead invest in various inflation-protected securities such as the Treasury TIPS, and other sovereign or corporate bonds that protect the investor against inflation. And these securities provide earnings in the form of interest and generally cost little or nothing to hold; often the securities dealer involved is willing to keep them at no cost, or the securities are just digital entries. This makes holding precious metals to overcome the implicit cost of inflation not rational.

Cryptocurrencies

Cryptocurrencies include several digital currencies, *Bitcoin* being one of the most famous. Since there is no limit on the number of different cryptocurrency brands (such as Bitcoin, Ethereum, EOS, and so on) that can be introduced to the market, one can expect sharp competition among them to keep the price appreciation of any particular brand in check. There is no model that tells us what the exchange rate between the different cryptocurrencies will be; the price behavior of Bitcoin supports this conclusion. From economic theory we can also expect that as the supply of all cryptocurrencies rises, their average value declines.

These currencies have no intrinsic value similar to, say gold's industrial value, other than the possibility that some people value being able to transfer funds by bypassing the banking system or avoiding government controls, and this aspect sets a lower bound on their value. How much is this attribute worth? Nobody knows. What we can say is that the dollar price of these currencies lies between a very low value to a high one. Economic theory also suggests that the price of a cryptocurrency is volatile and unforecastable.

Chapter 15

REAL ESTATE

Some 5% of Americans are farmers and many farmers invest in farmland. For the rest of us real estate investment is in housing and, more specifically, in houses that we live in. Investment in our houses constitute the major share of our investment portfolio. So, it is important to be informed about real estate investment, especially about housing.

Given the size and nature of the United States, it should be recognized that the housing market in America consists of numerous markets. The Pacific Coast real estate market (California, Oregon and Washington) is quite different from the real estate market in the Upper Midwest (parts of Michigan, Minnesota, Wisconsin, the Dakotas, Illinois, and Iowa). And these markets differ from the East Coast markets (New York, New Jersey, Massachusetts, Connecticut, and so on). The real estate markets of each of these and other regions can be quite distinct from one another. New York City's real estate market is rather different from the market in Rochester, NY. The Austin, TX, market is influenced by factors that may differ from factors that affect the Houston market. The same situation holds for the real estate markets in Europe. Given these differences, it is still useful to look at the broader real estate market since some of the important determinants of house prices apply to all markets.

For example, mortgage interest rates are nationwide and, in some cases, worldwide.

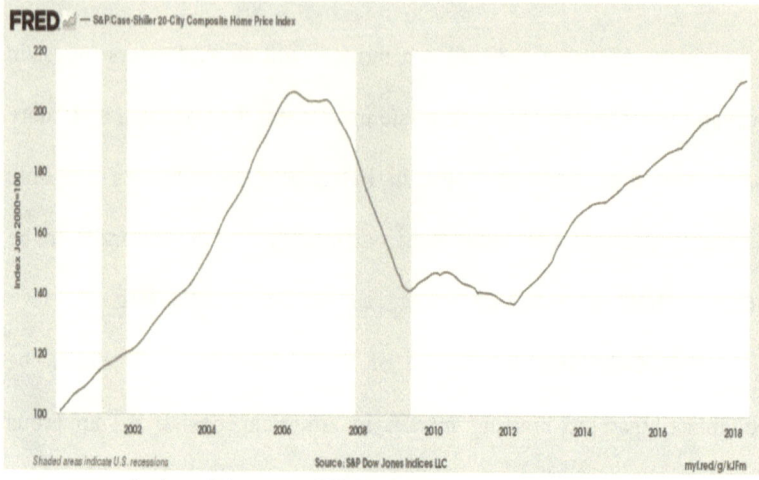

Index of Average US Home Prices, Year 2000=100

The above graph depicts the average home prices for the U.S. since 2000, with year 2000 price set at 100. The darker regions represent the two recessions the U.S. experienced since then. Notice that the recession of 2000 was brief (and mild), whereas the recession of 2008 lasted some two years and was severe; that is why it is called the Great Recession. Home prices reached their peak in 2006, at which point they were more than twice as high as they were six years earlier, rising by an average of 13% per year. Prices plunged by 1/3 by the end of the recession in late 2009 but continued their downward path, although not sharply, through 2012. They then resumed their upward trend to surpass their previous peak by early 2018.

This an annual increase of some 7.2%, not as fast as the go-go years of 2000-2006 but very high nevertheless.

As pointed out at the outset of this chapter, the US real estate market is diverse. Let's look at some individual markets. San Francisco home prices, one of the most expensive housing markets in the U.S., is shown in the graph below.

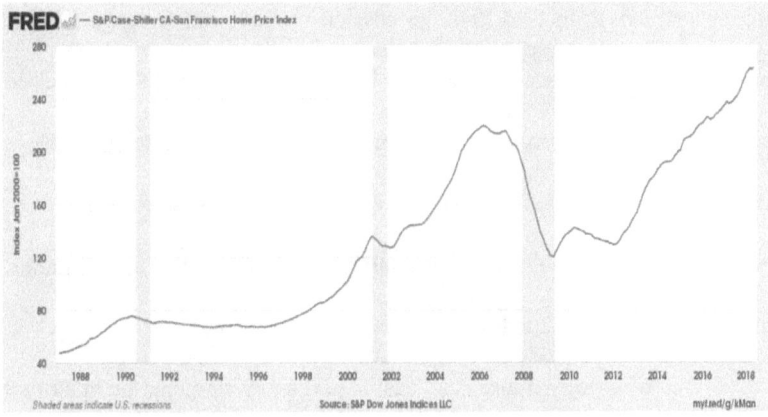

Index of Average San Francisco Housing Prices, Year 2000=100

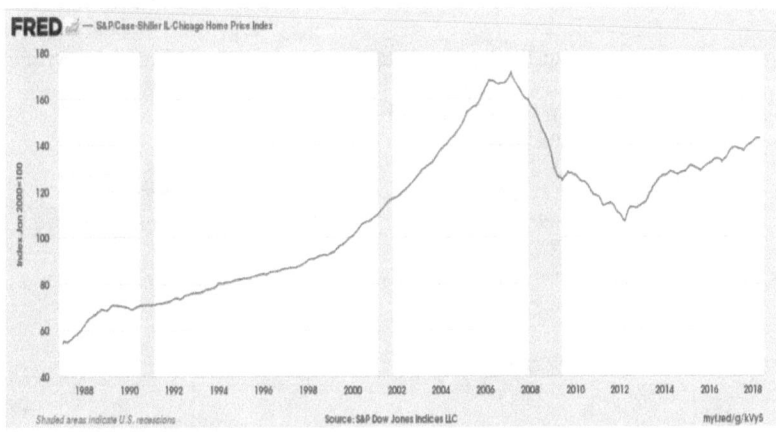

Index of Average Chicago Housing Prices, Year 2000=100

Observe the contrast between the two cities. First, note that while by 2018 San Francisco home prices are higher than the previous peak by some 13%, Chicago's prices are still about 17% below their previous peak. Second, from peak to trough, San Francisco homes lost about 45% of their value while Chicago lost much less at 35%. Third, during the Great Recession, San Francisco home prices fell by 35% but Chicago's home prices decline by a smaller 22%. And fourth, it appears that San Francisco home prices are more volatile than Chicago's. This is convincing evidence in support of the contention that real estate markets are diverse and local. Again, we come to the issue of risk and return. In real estate as in equities, higher return is associated with higher risk.

Since buying a house is at least in part an investment, the other part being a residence, then it is appropriate to compare the behavior of housing returns with returns one gets by investing in stocks. The table below summarizes returns and volatility of home prices in the U.S., Chicago and San Francisco, as well as for the S&P 500 index of stocks.

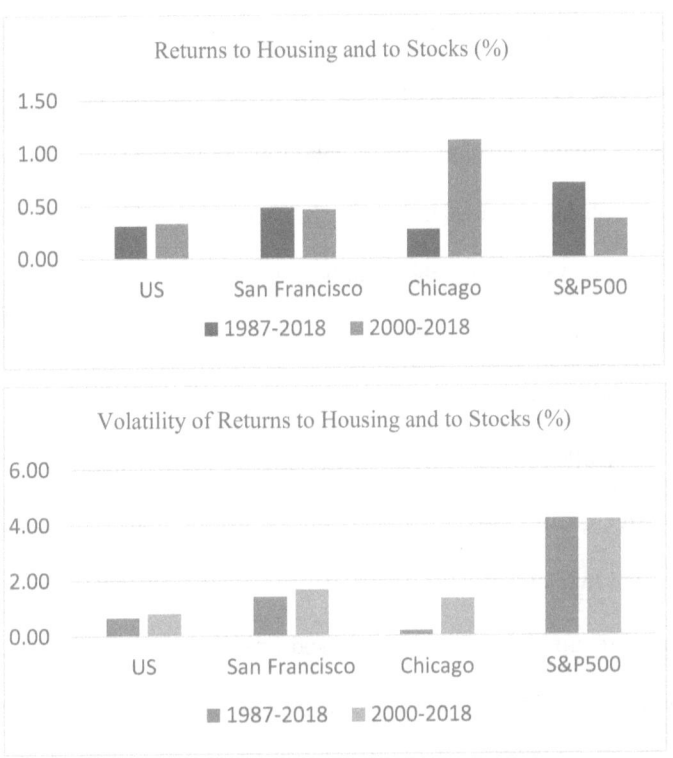

At the outset it should be mentioned that the return to housing is not entirely comparable to stock returns. The return to housing in this table considers only the change in the price of houses. All costs associated with homeownership such as taxes, maintenance, repairs, insurance, and utilities have been ignored. Of course, if markets were truly efficient and perfect, all these costs would be reflected in home prices. But the housing market is likely quite imperfect.

But the overall picture that emerges from the numbers in the table is supportive of the theory that when it comes to housing, just like securities, higher return is associated with higher risk. Both over the period since 1987 and since 2000 San Francisco housing has provided a higher return than Chicago housing but at significantly higher risk (as measured by the standard deviation, that is, volatility). In the 2000-2018 period, San Francisco's housing return volatility has been 25% greater than Chicago's. Worth noting too is that the volatility of return on housing has increased during 2000-2018 as compared with 1987-2018, while the return on stocks has stayed about the same.

Another aspect of housing investment should be addressed. A home mortgage qualifies for a tax break on the interest and real estate paid to state and municipality. Say you buy a house for $300,000. Assuming that you are required to pay 20% down and finance 80%, your mortgage loan is $240,000. With a 30-year loan, the interest rate on this mortgage will be around 4.3% per year, and your mortgage payments will be $14,250 per year. In the first few years, your total interest payment would be about $10,300 per annum. All of that is deductible from your income for tax purposes. If your average income tax rate is 15%, you save about $1,550 (15% × $10,300) from your taxes implying that your net mortgage cost will be $12,700, or about $1,050 per month. This may well beat renting a similar house, making home ownership attractive. In addition, real estate taxes are similarly tax deductible. At higher incomes and higher marginal tax rates home ownership becomes still more attractive. But keep in mind that there is a limit of how large the mortgage can be before tax breaks are eliminated.

It is worth noting that from the time San Francisco's housing reached their nadir by the middle of 2009 until the mid-2018, they had increased by a total of 144% while the S&P500 had increased by a total of 194%. Chicago home price increases did substantially worse than the stock market, by around 3.5% from their trough in mid-2011 to the mid-2018 versus 194% for the stock market. Even New York City housing prices appreciation fell substantially below the rise in the stock market.

Recent research across 16 industrialized countries (including the U.S., much of Western Europe and Australia) concludes that return to housing investment is similar to investment in stocks, but with less volatility than the latter. The figures in the table presented above suggest the same.

Finally, investment in a house means that you put a large fraction of your wealth in a form that is not liquid (i.e., you cannot sell at a fair market price speedily in case the need arises). You also end up with an investment that is not well-diversified which means that you are not compensated for the risk you take (see Chapter 9 for more detail).

Chapter 16

DERIVATIVES: OPTIONS, WARRANTS, FUTURES, SWAPS, and CDS

Options

Cars have become quite expensive these days. Even financing them often requires high monthly payments. The monthly payments are often quite a bit less if you lease a car. In addition to many requirements for leased cars, such as the number of miles you drive the car before a penalty is assessed, there is listed a terminal or *capitalized* value. This is the value that you are to pay to own the car at the end of the lease period. There is value to this arrangement: if the capitalized value is higher than the value you could sell the car for at lease's end, obviously you buy it at the capitalized value; even if you don't want the car, you can turn around and sell the car for more than what you paid for it. On the other hand, if the capitalized value is less than the market value you have two options. You can drop the car off at the dealership without owing anything (unless you have driven the car beyond the agreed-upon mileage or have done damage to the car). Alternatively, you can bargain with the dealership to bring the purchase price down below the capitalized value. In finance what is described in this situation involves an *option*. A lease with an "option" to buy gives the lessee the right to buy the car when the lease is up, and this makes the option valuable. Of course, dealers are aware of this and they try to capture this option value – sometimes they succeed, sometimes they don't.

Options provide the opportunity to take a position on stocks with little upfront cash investment. As the name implies, an option gives the owner of the option the right to do something without the obligation of doing so. Of course, when one party has the right to do something without being required to do so, there must be another party, called the *counter party*, who is obligated to make it possible for the first party to exercise that right. The owner of the option is in a great position, and in the financial markets to occupy such a position requires a payment. Who gets paid? The counterparty gets paid because she gives the first party this right; after all, it is the counterparty who has accepted the obligation to make good on the option. In real life, we encounter options often. For example, when a person asks another to marry him or her, the person asking gives the other person an option (to say yes or no). Often in renting a house or a store the contract specifies monthly rent, but the contract may also give the tenant the right to renew the lease or buy the property by a certain time for a given price; the counterparty is the (landlord) property owner. When leasing a car, the monthly lease payment is stated for the duration of the lease; at the end of the lease, the lessee usually has the right to buy the car at a predetermined price, which price (the "capitalized" value) is specified in the lease contract.

In the financial markets, options are issued on individual stocks as well on stock market indexes. There are also options on "futures" (futures are discussed below). Two kinds of option contracts exist: call options and put options. With an option one party has the right to do something without being obligated to do so; the other side of the option has the obligation without the right.

A *call option* gives the owner the right (but not the obligation) to <u>buy</u> an asset at a fixed price by (or at) a specified future date; the *put option* gives the owner the right (but not the obligation) to <u>sell</u> an asset at a fixed price by (or at) a specified future, *expiration*, date. The fixed price is called *strike* or *exercise* price. Options that can be exercised "by" a certain time are called "American"; those that can be exercised only "at" a certain time – i.e. not before or after – are called "European".

Creation of Options

How does the owner of an option acquire the option? She buys it from someone who sells it. As you would expect, the buyer pays the seller money for the option. This money compensates the seller for accepting the obligation and the associated inherent risk. Note that the exercise price of the asset involved in the option is fixed and there is a limit by which time the option can be exercised. The price of an option is called the *option premium*. It is common to say to *write* an option instead of to sell an option. Thus, the seller is the *writer* of the option. Where do options come from?

Investors themselves create options, independently of the company. There is a type of option the company issues (called *warrant*) to be discussed shortly. It is worth noting that options have no influence on the company's finances; the number of its shares outstanding or its cash flow are not affected.

Option Example

This example provides a detailed explanation of how options work. Tesla (TSLA) shares were priced at $352.45 at the close on August 9, 2018. A "call" option to buy a share of TSLA at a "strike" price of $350 was $6.50 with "expiration" date August 10, 2018. Strike prices that are exactly equal to closing prices are not often available since strike prices are offered in equal increments of whole numbers, such as those presented in the table below; for TSLA there was no strike price equal to its closing price. The "put" option with the same "strike" price of $350 and the same "expiration" date was worth $4.05. If you wanted to own the call option, you would have had to pay the issuer $6.50. Notice that although the option expires in one day, to own it one has to pay $6.50, even though the strike price of $350 is only $2.45 (=$352.45-350.00) less than the strike price. The reason is that TSLA share price may rise above not only the strike price but also above its current level of $352.45.

Now suppose that TSLA shares rise in value and close at $381. The call owner turns in his call option plus $350 (which is the strike price, not the current TSLA share price) and receives one share of TSLA. He can then turn around and sell his TSLA share for $380; his net profit is $380, less the $350 exercise price, less the $6.50 premium, for a total profit of $24.50. He invested $6.50 and ends up with $24.50 – this is the power of "leverage", the leverage that an option provides. How about the seller of the call? She pocketed the $6.50 premium and lost $31 on the stock, for a net loss of $24.50. The seller's loss includes the price $381 she could have obtained had she not given up the opportunity of selling her share (this is the opportunity cost). Observe that the loss of the seller of the option is exactly the same as the gain of the buyer of the option. This is always true with options. As a result, economists call option transactions *zero-sum games*. What if the writer of the option didn't own a share of TSLA? She can always buy it on the open market at $381; she would still lose the sum $24.50 on this transaction.

What if TSLA shares closed at something less than the strike price of $350? The option owner would choose not to exercise his option and just lose the $6.50 premium. Of course, the seller would not be required to hand in a share of TSLA to the call option owner either; the $6.50 premium is then her profit. Notice that once more the gain and loss of the two parties are equal in magnitude, for a zero net profit for the two of them.

Next consider the August 10, 2018, $350 put option that has a premium of $4.05. Assume that on August 10, 2018, TSLA shares close at $320. The owner of the put option can buy a share of TSLA for $320, give this share along with her put option to the seller and receive the exercise price of $350, for a net profit of 350 - 320 - 4.05 = $25.95. This is a stock that's worth only $320 so the seller of the option loses the $30 but he had already received the $4.05 premium, for a net loss of $25.95; again, the loss and the gain of the two parties sum to zero.

Tesla option prices at close, August 9, 2018. Tesla share price = 352.45

Expiration date: August 10, 2018

Price of Call, $	Strike Price, $	Price of Put, $
9.50	345	2.50
6.50	350	4.05
4.00	355	6.60
2.60	360	10.00

Tesla option prices at close, August 9, 2018. Tesla share price = 352.45

Expiration date: August 17, 2018

Price of Call, $	Strike Price, $	Price of Put, $
17.00	345	9.50
14.10	350	12.05
11.50	355	14.10
9.50	360	17.00

Note: all option prices are approximate; intermediate strike prices omitted for simplicity

Study these two tables carefully. First, look at the option prices in the top table for expiration on August 10. For call options, as the strike prices increase, the option premiums decline. And the exact opposite occurs for put options. Why? For call options, as the strike price rises, the opportunity to make money declines – so the call options become less valuable. The opposite is true for put options – they become more valuable as the strike price rises. Next, compare the option prices in the table for August 10 expiration with option premiums in the bottom table for expiration on August 17. All the prices for the August 17 expiration are higher than in the top table. Why? Because given more time the likelihood of hitting the strike price rises as time to expiration increases.

So now you have two of the properties of options:

(a) For calls, the premium (the option price) declines as <u>strike</u> price rises (or premium rises as strike price falls); for puts, the premium increases as strike price rises.

(b) For both calls and puts, as the time to <u>expiration</u> increases so does the option premium.

There are other determinants of option premiums:

(c) For both calls and puts, the option premium is higher the more <u>volatile</u> is the stock. The reason is that as volatility increases, the likelihood of hitting the strike price rises.

(d) For a given strike price, as the <u>stock price</u> rises, a call option gains value but a put option loses value. The reason is that for calls a rising stock price brings the strike price closer to stock price (if strike price was less than stock price) or exceeds the strike price, making the call more valuable. The opposite is true for a put option: the put option loses value when stock price rises.

(e) The payment of <u>dividends</u> reduces the value of the call option. This is because as we will see later (see section "Cash Dividends and Value of Stocks, in Chapter 18) with stock dividends, the stock loses value so the call loses value (as shown in 4. above). And since the stock loses value, its put option gains value.

(f) A rise in <u>interest rates</u> (just the risk-free rate – the US Treasury bills rate) causes call options to gain value but put options to lose value. The reason is that a higher interest rate reduces the present value of the strike price (this follows from 1. above).

You may wonder that since so many common factors such as volatility, stock price, and so on affect the prices of both calls and puts, shouldn't there be a close connection between call and put options? You would be right; there is a connection and it is called the *put-call parity*. Specifically, the relationship is:

Put value = call value – current stock price + PV of strike price

– PV of dividends

where PV stands for "present value"; for most situations, the most important factors are the current share price and the stock's volatility. It turns out that on August 8 the shares of TSLA became terribly volatile due to some statements the CEO, Elon Musk, made about taking Tesla private.

The next question you may ask is what determines the exact value of either the put or the call option? Well, two economists came up with the formula to calculate the value of options. One of them, Myron Scholes won the Nobel Prize in economics; the other, Fischer Black, died young and the Nobel prize is not given posthumously. The Black-Scholes formula (sometimes called Black-Scholes-Merton model since Robert Merton also developed a formula to calculate option prices) is named after them. You can buy the formula and it is available for calculators.

As an aside, Scholes, Merton (another Nobel laureate) and a few other brilliant economists and investors formed a hedge fund called Long-Term Capital Management (LTCM). They were making pennies on *market mispricing* (especially on bonds) but using tens of millions of dollars of borrowed money (as leverage); for a time they were fabulously successful so they attracted billions in funds. Unfortunately, the market stopped behaving as they expected so LTCM went spectacularly bankrupt. To save the financial institutions that had invested in LTCM, the Fed stepped in. (Why do the Fed and the government always save the big guys – as in 2007-2008 --but if you go broke you are on your own?)

There are various ways in which options can be used to enhance earnings or reduce investment risk. You can protect your investment against a downturn in stocks by owning put options. Put options gain value as stock prices go down, so if your stocks lose value the put options on those stocks gain value – this is how puts offer protection against falling share prices. But remember this protection comes at a price, the price (the option premium) you pay to acquire the options.

Suppose you own a stock whose value has increased quite a bit and you don't expect its price to rise further. You can sell the shares. Alternatively, you can sell calls on your stock and receive the option premium and make money on your stock on top of any dividends that you may receive. If your prediction turns out as you expected, the calls expire unexercised and you still own the shares; you can repeat the game or sell your shares on the market. The risk is that the stock price drops below what you could have sold the shares instead of selling (writing) calls on them.

Let's say you want to buy some stock. You can buy the shares outright. Alternatively, you can sell put options with exercise price below the current market price of the shares. You receive the premium now and if the share price drops to below the strike price the owner of the puts will exercise the options and force you to buy the shares at the strike price; this price will be lower than the current market price that you were willing to buy them. Of course, the risk is that had you waited and not sold the puts you would be in a position to buy the shares for less.

Here's another way you could use options. TSLA shares sell at $352.45. You expect these shares to move but you don't know in which direction. You could buy both the 355 call and 345 put options expiring

August 17 for $11.50 and $9.50, respectively. If, say, the stock moves to $380 your call option is worth $35; your net gain is then 35-11.50-9.50 = $14.00 (because your put expires worthless). Next suppose that you expect the TSLA shares to remain in the range of $345 and $355; your strategy would then be to sell both the 355 call and the 345 put options because both will expire worthless if your forecast is correct. There are other strategies one can follow depending on your forecast regarding the levels and volatility of stocks.

There are many situations where options are involved in financial transactions although the options are not obvious. When a broker guarantees a minimum price for an asset you want him to sell for you, he has sold you a put option. If the asset sells for more than the guaranteed price, you do not exercise the put; if it sells for less than the guaranteed price, you get the guaranteed price – which is equivalent to saying that you exercise the put.

Warrants

A *warrant* is a call option a company issues on its stock. Just like a call option, a warrant gives the right, but not the obligation, to buy one or more shares in the company at a certain price at or by a certain time. Warrants are usually attached to shares or bonds the company issues. While ordinary call options have no effect on the company's cash flow or the number of share outstanding, warrants affect both. When the holder of a warrant exercises it, the company must issue new stock. The reason warrants are issued is to make the stock or bonds the warrants are attached to more attractive, that is, increase their value (and price) to investors: that is how warrants impact the firm's cash flow.

Forwards and Futures

You go to a car dealership and want to buy this beautiful Italian electric deep yellow sports car that can go from 0 to 60 in 3.5 seconds and come to full stop at 60 mph in 14 feet; it sells for $19,596. Great buy but, alas, the dealer doesn't have this car on the lot but can get it in 18 days. You agree to buy this car by making a deposit of $40 and pay the full price upon delivery in 18 days. Both you and the dealership have obligated yourselves to fulfill this contract. This is an example of a *forward* contract. Observe the difference between this forward contract and the option. With an option, one party is obligated to do something while the other party has the choice of doing something. With a forward contract both parties are obligated, one party to deliver an asset at some pre-determined future time, and the other party must pay the agreed-upon price upon delivery of the asset. The asset is known, its price is fixed as is the delivery time.

Suppose now that the next day the price of the euro (the currency used in Italy) goes up from $1.16 per euro to $1.22, an increase of 5.2%. And you find out that the price of cars similar to the one you just "bought" has gone up to $20,380 – by about 4% since the Italian manufacturer decides that it will eat some of the higher cost to keep it competitive. You could sell your "forward" contract with the dealer to a friend for a profit of $784. This is how investors earn a profit on forward contracts. If instead the euro falls, your forward contract's value decline to less than $19,596 and if you try to sell it you would lose money, because the dealer would hold you to the original price of $19,596. In fact, if you decided to back out of the deal (because the price of the car has fallen) the dealership could hold you to the original contract, causing you to lose money on the deal.

Here's another example. You are planning a trip to Europe in one month and you need 850 euros. You ask your bank to have the euros ready for you to pick up in three weeks. The bank will charge you 1.16 per euro for a total of $986. This is again a forward contract: the bank will deliver €850 in three weeks and you will give the bank the agreed-upon price of $986.

A *futures* contract is exactly like a forward contract in concept, except that futures contracts are standardized and traded on (organized) exchange markets. This means that the size of the contracts and the delivery dates are fixed; furthermore, the parties to the futures contracts do not generally know each other. The exchange also provides a mechanism that provides a guarantee that the contract will be honored.

Futures contracts are quite popular and used by businesses often. For example, airlines buy and sell fuel futures; refiners buy and sell crude oil futures; farmers engage in agricultural product futures; and so on.

Futures are often used to forecast actual asset prices at some point in the future. People some time use futures to forecast the outcome of elections. The University of Iowa, years ago, established a computerized futures market as a training and research tool. By pooling the forecasts of investors, it attempts to predict election outcomes.

Spot, Forward and Futures Prices

In financial markets, there are often two sets of prices: *forward* or *futures prices* and *spot prices*. When you go to the market and buy a pound of peanuts for $2.65, the price $2.65 is a spot price. With the car example, the dealer agreed to deliver the car in 18 days and receive $19,596 at delivery time; this is a forward transaction. Suppose that you don't want to wait so the dealer gets on the phone and finds another dealer who has the car you want for delivery now, for a price of $20,600. The $20,600 is the spot price and the $19,596 is the forward price. If the item in question was trading on an organized futures market, it would be a futures price.

Similarly, as discussed in Chapter 12, we distinguish between spot and forward (as well as futures) interest rates.

Credit Default Swaps (CDS)

A CDS is nothing but insurance on the default risk of a loan or a bond. When initially introduced, the CDS was an insurance policy to permit the lender to buy protection against the borrower's default risk; if the borrower defaulted, the CDS covered the loss. Thus, the credit worthiness of the issuer of the CDS (that is, the insurer) substituted for the credit worthiness of the borrower. If the borrower's credit rating was BB (relatively low) and a JP Morgan with a credit rating AAA (very high), and JP Morgan insured the loan via a CDS, then the lender was quite certain that the loan was safe from default. Over time, however, CDSs became an instrument that investors could use to speculate on the financial condition of particular issuers.

During the financial crisis of the Great Recession of 2008, the value of the CDSs shot up due to the fear that borrowers would default on a large scale while at the same time the issuers of CDSs were averse to insure loans; therefore, these issuers were demanding higher "insurance premiums". It is estimated that by 2008 some $63-trillion of CDSs were outstanding (for comparison, the US GDP amounted to one-fifth of that at around $14-trillion). By 2017, the value of CDSs outstanding stood at around $10-trillion. The insurance company AIG was a significant issuer of CDSs, particularly on subprime mortgages and other loans.

The way it works, in its simplest form, is as follows. The Entity B borrows $1 million from the lending Bank L. Bank L in turn buys insurance against default by Entity B from CDS seller S. Bank L pays a fee (similar to an insurance premium) every three months to CDS seller S (the "insurance company"), until either there is default or the loan made to Entity B matures. In the event of default by Entity B, CDS seller S will pay the Bank L the principal value of the loan, $1 million in this case. In 2009-2010 these insurance fees rose by many times, to as high as 200 times their pre-2008 levels in some cases, such as on loans made to the governments of Portugal, Spain, and Greece.

Swaps

A *swap*, as the name suggests, involves the exchange of two securities or other assets, such as bonds or foreign exchange, between two parties. To illustrate, you have a bond with a principal (face value) of $10,000 with fixed coupon (interest) rate of 6% per year; the bond matures in 10 years. You expect short-term interest rates to go higher. You find someone who prefers the fixed 6% per year for ten years to short term rates that can be variable. The two of you agree to exchange the interest on $10,000. You pay the second party 6% per year – that is, $600 per year – and receive from her whatever the short-term rate prevails each year. Why would the second party want to agree to this swap? She exchanges a variable and hence risky interest for the certainty of 6%.

When the Fed wants to cause a change in the quantity of money in the economy for a short period, it uses swaps. The Fed may buy a

Treasury security from a bank but agree to sell that security back to the bank at a certain time in the near future for a predetermined price. The first step involves swapping cash for a security; the second step reverses the swap – hence the term *reverse swap*. The first step increases the quantity of money in the banking system which in turn may increase the amount of money in the <u>economy</u>. The second step withdraws cash from the system.

Consider an American company that sells goods to a Chinese business every month and it is promised to be paid in yuan. There is another company that buys Chinese goods and pays it in US dollars. The two American businesses can swap these payments: the company selling to the Chinese business will then receive dollars from the firm that buys Chinese goods, and the latter receives the yuan to pay the Chinese business.

Chapter 17

INVESTMENT VEHICLES

There are a number of different financial institution engaged in various aspects of securities. This chapter discusses some of the most important of these institutions. These companies are in some ways like industrial corporations. Industrial corporations raise funds from shareholders and invest the proceeds in plant and equipment to produce products; these products are the source of profits for the shareholders. Investment companies raise funds from individuals and other institutions and invest them in securities. The earnings from these securities are the source of their profits. Investment companies are organized to meet different financial objectives.

Mutual Funds

Open-end mutual funds or simply *mutual funds* (MuF) are in the business of making money by receiving your money and investing it in securities in your behalf. For this service they charge a fee, the source of their income. MuFs sell shares to investors and redeem shares on demand at what is called *net asset value* (NAV). MuFs use the money they raise to invest in a portfolio of securities, generally a well-diversified portfolio. The NAV is simply the value of the portfolio per share. As a MuF sells and redeems shares, the number of its shares outstanding changes all the time.

A mutual fund's NAV is calculated after the market closes and it is only then that the MuF shares are transacted, even though an investor can place orders at any time during or after market hours. There are about 8,000 MuFs in the U.S. with net assets of $19 trillion.

Mutual funds may follow one of two approaches to investing. First, there are those that take a *passive* position, which is to buy essentially a basket of stocks that mimic either the entire stock market or a sector of the market and leave this basket pretty much unchanged for a long time. In *sector investing*, the mutual fund may focus on transportation, biotechnology, high-tech, commodities and so on. They could of course invest in every stock that is listed on the market, for example, in the stocks included in the S&P500. The objective here is to match the overall market. This approach is a low-cost way of investing, with little money spent on research to find out which stock is a good investment and which is not. Accordingly, the fees charged by these funds tend to be relatively low, in the 0.1%-0.3% of invested funds. Just recently a major fund announced that it has set up a new fund that has zero expense; there is no charge whatsoever for investing in this fund. Is this significant? Consider a very low-cost fund that charges $1.40 per $1,000 capital per year. If you save and invest $1,000 per year in real terms (i.e., adjusted for inflation) for thirty years in a zero-cost fund versus this low-cost fund, you save yourself $800 over that period. If you invest $10,000 per year, your saving amounts to nearly $8,000, not an insignificant sum.

The alternative to the passive investing mutual funds are those funds that claim that they can beat the market by being good stock pickers or good at timing the market; they are *active* funds. These funds charge much higher fees, ranging as high as perhaps 3%-4% of invested funds. One justification they offer is that it is costly to do research to discover stocks with high price growth potential and to hire the persons with the skill to identify such stocks requires the payment of high salaries. It is true that research is expensive and people who claim they have the "right" skills command high remuneration. The cost these funds incur is irrelevant. The important question is "can these funds increase the return on your investment" – that is, do these funds beat the market consistently, and so far the answer seems to be in the negative. Remember this: when the stock market returns something like an average of 6%-7% annually, active funds must earn returns in the 9%-10% range to justify their fees. Even Mr. Buffet's Berkshire Hathaway was unable to earn close to 9% per year in the past decade or so (during late 2007 through mid-2018).

Exchange Traded Funds (ETF)

In the past few years a new way of investing in funds has been introduced; these are the *exchange-traded funds* or *ETF*s; we'll discuss these in more detail shortly but for now what is important to know is that ETFs are very low cost, charging less than 0.1% of invested funds. ETFs are also mutual funds and they too specialize in the overall market or specific sectors of the market, just like mutual funds. There are already a number of marijuana ETFs and their number is certain to increase as cannabis becomes more widely legal and more companies enter the business of growing and distributing marijuana.

More cannabis ETFs will come to the market

There are some important differences between ordinary mutual funds (MuF) and exchange-traded funds (ETF). When you want to buy or sell shares in a MuF you place your order at any time that's convenient for you, even in the middle of the night. But your order will not be executed until the market closes after you have placed your order. Let's say it is

Thursday 11:00 a.m. New York time when you place your order to buy 100 shares of a MuF; this order won't be executed until the market closes at 4:00 p.m. The reason is that the MuF has to wait until the market closes for the MuF to calculate the value of all the securities it has in its portfolio to come up with the value of the portfolio; in turn, that determines the price of each share in the MuF, its NAV.

With ETFs, the value of the portfolio of the ETF is calculated continuously so that its NAV is known at every point in the time. Accordingly, if you place your order to buy 100 shares of an ETF at 11:00 a.m. it will be executed immediately. This is a highly valuable attribute. Suppose that you observe that the stock market is slipping and you decide to liquidate your position in a MuF and an ETF before things get worse. With the ETF your position is closed immediately and you will have cash in your account. With the MuF you have to wait until the market closes and, therefore, watch the value of your shares in the MuF perhaps fall further.

ETFs offer additional advantages compared to MuFs. You can sell an ETF *short* or buy it on *margin* (see below for short sales and margin buying), something not allowed by law for MuFs.

There are additional things to consider when deciding to go with an ETF or a MuF, and that has to do with taxes. When you sell a stock whose price has risen, you have to pay a capital gains tax. Suppose that a MuF has two stocks in its portfolio: ABC and XYZ. The MuF decides that

ABC has run its price increase course and should be sold and replaced by stock KLM. You as a holder of the shares of the MuF incur the capital gains tax. But the ETF, by law, can simply exchange its shares of ABC for shares of KLM without any tax consequences.

Next consider the costs associated with buying and selling ETFs and MuFs. With ETFs there is a bid-ask spread – meaning that the price you pay when buying it is greater than the price the dealer paid for it, similar to buying and selling any stock. With MuFs there is no bid-ask spread. So to this extent there is the benefit of investing in MuFs instead of investing in ETFs. But we just saw that ETFs are more *tax efficient*. Thus, there is a tradeoff between tax efficiency and the bid-ask spread. Which investment path is better depends on the type of ETF and MuF, and your investment holding period. In some equity investments, the tax advantage of an ETF covers the bid-ask spread cost. With some bond investments, it may take two years before the tax efficiency of an ETF can cover the bid-ask spread cost.

Closed-End Funds

Closed-end funds (CEF) are investment companies that even more closely resemble industrial companies. They raise funds and use them to invest in a portfolio of securities. They then issue a fixed number of shares, as do industrial corporations. These shares are subsequently bought and sold among investors without the CEF's involvement; therefore, unlike the

MuFs, the number of shares outstanding of CEFs do not change. The price of these shares can change without necessarily a close correlation with the NAV of the portfolio. In fact, there is often a difference between the market price of a CEF's shares and its NAV. There have been occasions when the share price of a CEF has far exceeded its NAV – which doesn't make sense since one could buy the portfolio in the CEF's for much less on the open market.

Real Estate Investment Trusts (REITs)

Real estate investment trusts (REIT) are closed-end funds that invest in real estate companies and in mortgages. REITs raise equity capital by issuing shares; but they also raise capital by borrowing from banks or issuing bonds. They tend to be heavily leveraged, with a debt ratio of 70% being the norm. REITs are often established by mortgage companies, insurance companies and banks.

Money Market Mutual Funds

Money market mutual funds (MMMF) are investment firms that invest in securities with an original maturity of less than one year. These provide an alternative to interest-bearing deposits at commercial banks; however, funds invested in MMMFs are not insured (deposits with banks are insured up to a limit of $250,000, as discussed earlier), although such deposits have proven quite safe. The exception to this was when the

Primary Reserve Fund shares "broke the buck", that is, fell below $1, meaning that shareholders lost part of their investment. This was the first time ever that the share price of a MMMF dipped below $1. When this happened there was a run on MMMFs and investors started pulling money out of these funds. To stop the run the US Treasury stepped in and extended insurance to all the MMMF accounts; this insurance lasted for one year, through September 18, 2009.

Unit Investment Trusts

Unit investment trusts (UIT) have some characteristics in common with both mutual funds and closed-end funds. They issue redeemable shares, called "units", as do mutual funds. The number of shares issued is fixed, similar to closed-end funds. However, unlike mutual and closed-end funds, UIT's units mature at which time the portfolio is liquidated and the proceeds are distributed among the shareholders. UITs generally have fixed portfolios of relatively few (around 20) stocks or bonds with little or no change over the life of the UIT.

Hedge Funds

Hedge funds, similar to mutual funds, invest their clients' funds. But only "eligible" individuals (generally these are wealthy people) and institutional investors are accepted as clients. Hedge funds are lightly regulated and, therefore, have great latitude in their investment strategy.

Furthermore, they can change their strategy as they deem warranted. They tend to pursue complex investment strategies expecting to beat the market. Hedge funds share in the profits of their investments, often taking 20% of the profits earned. This is in addition to the management fee they charge, usually around 1%-2% of investment capital.

Investment in a hedge fund tends to be rather illiquid compared to mutual funds and ETFs. Hedge funds require the investors to leave their money with the funds for an extended period, often years, because the hedge funds themselves tend to invest in long-term assets. Returns on illiquid assets require additional returns as compensation.

Hedge funds focus on achieving as high an *alpha* as possible. Alpha measures the return on investment that exceeds what the riskiness of the portfolio warrants. Hedge funds have generally managed to earn high returns, even after charging high fees. Their strategy is to take both *long and short* positions simultaneously. A long position assumes that the prices of securities will rise while a short position assumes that prices will fall. The long position is achieved by, for example, buying the securities or buying call options; the short position involves selling the securities or buying puts. The short position protects the long position in case security prices fall. There is evidence suggesting that hedge funds are successful in beating the market. This can be a consequence of the securities markets not being perfectly efficient, allowing mispricing that clever investors can take advantage of. Some have argued that they achieve the higher returns because their investments are exposed to risks that are not measured. The high returns could also reflect the fact that clients' investments are illiquid.

One very famous hedge fund was Long Term Capital Management (LTCM), set up by some Nobel Laureate economists and other financial luminaries. LTCM bought less liquid assets and sold more liquid assets; less liquid assets are cheaper so LTCM made money by "selling liquidity", earning money this way. LTCM was enormously profitable and presumably well-hedged and not subject to serious risk of losing based on historical experience. It earned better than 40% on its investments in its few years in existence. But an unforeseen event appeared in 1998: Russia defaulted on its sovereign (government) debt, creating a liquidity crisis. Such highly rare events are referred to as "black swan" risk (because prior to the discovery of Australia and its black swans the belief in the world was that swans were always white). LTCM lost $550 million in just one day and its losses kept mounting, imperiling the financial system. The fund was liquidated with the intervention of the Federal Reserve.

Private Equity

A *private equity* is also an investment firm, not publicly traded, organized as a limited partnership. Investors in private equities are institutional investors such as university funds, pension funds, wealthy individuals, etc. These firms raise equity funds as well as debt to make investments. Most often the private equities purchase companies, reorganize them and make changes to increase their value. Once that objective is achieved, the private equities sell the companies.

Private equities also fund venture capital firms which in turn, finance new ventures.

Venture Capital

Established companies can raise needed funds by going to the stock and bond markets to issue new securities. New businesses without much track records and unknown to the securities markets do not have access to these markets. To grow and become established these businesses rely for funding on specialized investment groups who assist these ventures. These are *venture capital* (VC) funds and are usually organized as limited partnerships. They tend to specialize by industry and their managers are experienced and well-connected. In addition to funding, they help manage the new ventures and find the appropriate human resources to make the venture a success. VCs take equity in the ventures they finance and sometimes extend them loans. The source of VC funding are wealthy individuals who invest in them. VCs support the ventures with the objective to bring them to the market through an IPO (initial public offering) or sell them to other companies.

There are about 1,000 VCs in the U.S., employing some 7,000 people. VC investments are not diversified. The returns to VC investors are highly skewed and a portion of the returns owes to illiquidity of investment in VCs. Many of the ventures fail; only a few turn out to offer fantastic profits – only a few become Google and Facebook.

Angel Investors

These are wealthy individuals and groups of wealthy individuals who provide initial funding for new ventures at the very beginning, often when the venture is at the "idea" stage. The amount of funds the individual angel investors provide is quite small, often as little as $5,000 and seldom as high as $100,000. The angel groups, which are organized by several individuals, may offer up to $1-$1.5 million for startups. Angels are crucial in helping startups; they have funded approximately 70,000 new ventures.

The returns earned by angel investors are quite lopsided. Better than one-half end up losing money on their investments. Only about 7% receive some 90 per cent of the earnings.

Crowd Funding

This is a relatively new mechanism for funding startups. Most individuals can invest in startups through this mechanism. However, there are legal restrictions in how crowd funds can raise money.

Pension Funds

Pension funds collect what individuals save and invest these savings in the financial markets to be liquidated at a later date to cover the pensions of the retirees. In this they are similar to insurance companies and mutual funds. Pension funds differ from the latter in that they offer individuals tax-deferred savings during their working years; the retiree pays taxes on these savings when he or she withdraws money from the account. There are currently nearly 700,000 pension funds in the United States, and households have about one-third of their financial assets invested in these funds.

There are two types of pension funds. Private pension funds are those that are administered by private companies. Public pension funds are those that are administered by the federal, a state or a local government. Social Security is a pension fund administered by the federal government. As of 2017, pension fund reserves were well over $27 trillion; the various public pension funds amount to about one-third of the total.

A pension is either a *defined contribution* fund or a *defined benefit* fund. Many government-sponsored pensions are of the defined benefit variety, while many privately-sponsored pensions are of the defined contribution type. With a defined benefit pension the employer promises to pay the pensioner a fixed amount, depending on her earnings and years of service – e.g., $50 per $10,000 annual earnings, for each year of service. In contrast, a defined contribution provides no guarantee on the amount of the pension received; the employer contributes a specified amount during the employee's working years. The employee himself can also contribute toward his pension. A 401k plan is an example of a defined contribution pension. A defined contribution plan usually allows the employee to direct, subject to certain restrictions, where the funds should be invested.

Many employers, both public and private, have been moving away from defined benefits in favor of defined contribution plans. Many public pensions are underfunded currently; that is one reason for preferring the defined contribution option. Most state and local government pension plans are funded on a "pay as you go" basis: what is collected from current <u>employees</u> is paid to current <u>retirees</u>. As the number of retirees rises relative to the number of current employees, the contribution by current employees fails to cover pension payments.

Private pension plans are regulated under the Employee Retirement Income Security Act of 1974 (ERISA). To be eligible for tax-deferred status, the plan must meet certain standards under this Act. ERISA also established the Pension Benefit Guarantee Corporation (PBGC) that provides insurance for defined <u>benefit</u> pension fund participants. The PBGC steps in if the pension plan is unable to meet its promised obligations.

Ponzi Schemes or Pyramids

Since so many people everywhere in the world have invested in schemes that have come to be known as *Ponzi* or *pyramids* and lost money, it is essential to discuss them briefly here. A Ponzi or pyramid is a scheme to collect money from investors hoping to earn abnormally high returns without little or no risk; the outcome of these schemes is that invariably the investors get burned, losing all or nearly all their money. Basically, the way it works is as follows: the schemer collects money from a group promising them high returns; he then collects more money from another group in a subsequent period. Part of the second group's money is given to the first group as investment "return" on their funds, but a good part is kept (and spent) by the schemer. The schemer now needs to raise more money from a third group to pay the first and the second groups, and so on for additional investors. Pretty soon, of course, the schemer finds it more and more difficult to attract new investors as the number of new investors becomes smaller and smaller. Finally, the schemer runs out of investors to give him money, and for him to pay off previous investors. The Ponzi scheme ends with a few early winners and lots of losers.

Here's an example of a Ponzi scheme that is similar to some real ones. You, Ms. A, sell gadgets. You find 2 other salespeople, Mr. B1 and Mr. B2, to sell your gadgets. To sell your gadgets you charge them each $50 for the gadgets that cost you only $25 to produce. So right away you have made 2 x $25 = $50. The latter two salesmen can now find 2 persons each, C1, C2, C3 and C4, and sell the gadgets to them for $50 per gadget. B1 and B2 must now buy 4 gadgets from A at $50 per gadget so A gets 4 x $50 = $200 from B1 and B2; but B1 and B2 get a commission of, say, $25 per gadget sold. Thus, A pays $50 each to B1 and B2 for a total of $100; A nets $100. B1 and B2 have recouped their original $50 paid to A. Next round involves each C to recruit 2 people for a total of 8 people. The Cs can make money only if they can sell gadgets to other recruits D – each must recruit at least 2 new salespeople. As this process progresses, the number of people that must be recruited rises exponentially. Every round requires a doubling of the number of recruits. In round 15 you need nearly 33,000 people. In round 18 the number jumps to 262,000. In round 25 you need 34-million people – that is just about the combined populations of Hungary, the Czech Republic, Slovakia, and Belarus, or the entire population of California. Is it wonder that pyramid schemes fail ultimately? And the losers are invariably the large number of late-comers.

Charles Dickens mentioned such a scheme in the 1840s. Sarah Howe used it in the 1880s. The scheme is named after Charles Ponzi who used it extensively in the 1920s. Interestingly, Mr. Ponzi started out as a legitimate investor but then discovered that it was easier and more remunerative to cheat avaricious people using the Ponzi scheme. More recently, Bernard Madoff, previously the head of the Nsadaq, pulled off a gigantic Ponzi worth some $65-billion. Madoff promised investors returns that were just too good to be true but greed is blind (just like love!).

Investors often begged Madoff to accept their money! Madoff simply cooked the books to show there were gains where none existed. He did the old fashion thing: collect money from the later investors to pay the early ones, and to himself and to his family. He led a fabulously rich life style. A financial analyst, Harry Markopolos claims that it took him four minutes to determine that Madoff's investment claims were impossible; he warned the SEC in 1999 of his finding that Madoff was a fraud but no one there took his portent seriously. Madoff's fraud was eventually discovered and he admitted guilt in 2009; Madoff was sentenced to 150 years in prison – 150 years was then the maximum sentence for his crime.

If something sounds too good to be true it probably isn't.

Chapter 18

HUMAN CAPITAL: A PERSON'S EARNING POWER

Earnings Time Profile

A baby is born. He or she is totally dependent on the mother and the mother may receive assistance from her partner. In particular, not only is baby not earning any income, the baby has negative earning since he or she only consumes. This situation continues well into the child's early teenage years. Even if the young person gets a job, such as babysitting or delivering newspapers, he or she earns very little, not enough even to feed herself or himself. But as the teenager goes to school and receives an education, she/he acquires some skills and understands her or his environment, the teenager experiences improved earning potential. For example, the teenager may now get a job bagging groceries or help sorting packages for mail-order businesses. Many such jobs require certain skills that a person with little or no education lacks.

Education, academic or vocational, provides necessary skills that increase a person's ability to earn a higher income. This is the idea of *human capital*: money is invested in a person and that investment yields returns in the form of higher income and perhaps even better jobs. Up to the time of early teenage years, it is the parents who provide the funds to invest in a young person, sometimes with some sort of help or subsidy by the government.

After high school, one can attend college or a vocational school. If the parents are rich, they pay, in full or in part, the cost of getting this education. A student may also receive financial aid from various sources. Otherwise the student may work to pay for her or his education. Regardless of the source of the funds, money is being invested in the student and the education increases the student's human capital. The next thing is for a person to get a job or start a business. Over time, a person becomes more proficient at a job or running a business, resulting in higher earnings for the person. At some point, a person's expertise may become dated and less valuable. The person's human capital, like a physical capital such as equipment or structure depreciates over time. A person must update and upgrade her expertise by investing more in her human capital. As the world transforms more rapidly, this reinvestment must occur more frequently.

Eventually a person decides to retire. This decision can come about for various reasons. Illness, old age, family issues hasten the decision.

Let us recapitulate the earnings profile from birth to old age. At very young age, one earns net negative income. In the early teenage years minimal income can be earned. Earnings rise after high school, even if one decides to stop one's formal education, because of socialization, maturity and work experience.

Attending college or vocational school is expensive. Acquiring more post-high school education often results in negative *net* earnings –

i.e., whatever one earns at work, less the cost of attending school. This can be viewed as investment in a person's human capital.

When a person leaves school and engages in a full-time job, the person's earnings rise sharply and, as discussed above, keep rising over the years. But at some point a person's income turns down due to the inadequacy of the person's skills falling short of the new work requirements. Earnings drop to zero at retirement. The retiree draws on the savings that she accumulated while employed at a job or the income she earned in her business.

The plot of the time profile of a typical person's income over the lifetime is depicted below:

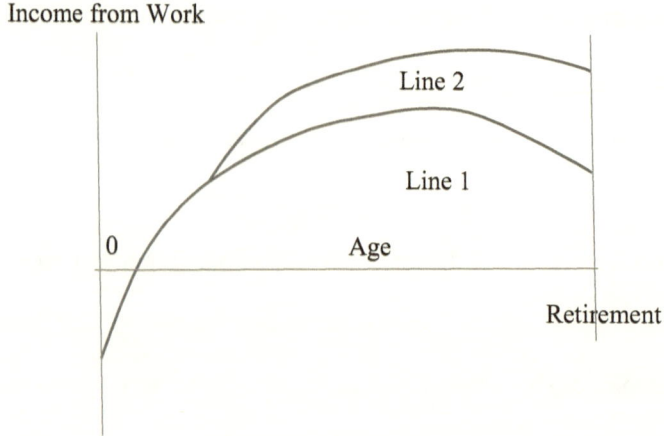

Without upgrading one's capabilities, one's earning time profile may look like Line 1. Upgrading one's skills changes the lifetime earnings to resemble Line 2. Of course, this upgrading can be a continuous process, in which case the line keeps shifting up over time.

Education and Training

Finishing high school results in lifetime earnings far higher than going through life without a high-school degree or a GED. College education leads to much higher average lifetime earnings than completing only high school. Vocational education, similarly, results in higher lifetime income.

Education and skill increase the value of human capital and income

Acquiring skills is an <u>investment</u> since it requires spending funds that you could have saved and invested in financial or real assets. Instead, you <u>invest the time</u> that you could have spent earning an income. One of the costs of getting an education or learning skills is this foregone income, the opportunity cost of education.

I once had a student majoring in finance but the student was doing poorly. I met with the student and inquired the reason why the student's work was so inadequate. The response was that the student did not like finance but preferred a career in wedding planning. Such a student will never do well in a career in finance. One should pursue one's passions; we all have multiple passions and aptitudes and at least one of the skills associated with these passions will bring us success and happiness.

From all the evidence we have it seems that education and training, college or vocational, have a return much higher than investment in equities. One estimate suggests that each <u>additional</u> year of training or education increases one's <u>annual</u> income by 10% for ever, versus about 5% to 7% in returns on equities. If you are earning $40,000 per year, an additional year of training or education adds $4,000 <u>per year</u> during your lifetime of work – this is substantial. If you work for forty years, this amounts to $1.6 million (of course, taxes will eat into the $1.6 million but what's left over can still buy a nice house). It should be added that training and education also provide some degree of protection against competition with the less-skilled foreign workers in a globalized economy.

Professional Athletes (and Other Stars)

Sometimes renewing and enhancing a particularly remunerative skill is not possible. This applies predominantly to professional athletes (as well as to some stars in the arts world). These athletes have rare abilities either endowed to them by nature (or god) or acquired due to extreme training and encouragement from early childhood. For example, to become a first-rate basketball player the individual must be taller than the population average and be trained when very young. To become a great quarterback, the player must be tall, have a strong arm, and possess a very particular type of mental acuity. A major league baseball hitter must be strong as well as a fast runner. These athletes usually have a very short career in their sport but earn very high incomes during that brief career.

The average career of a National Football League (NFL) player is quite short at 3 years. But since many members of the NFL never even start playing, excluding the non-players means that a player's career is around 10-11 years (those nominated to the pro-bowl play an average of 12 years). In 2018, the average salary of an NFL player was around $2.7 million, although some top players earned nearly ten times that average. The lowest salary is around $500,000 per year. Since the average player starts at the age of about 20, even after 10 years, the retiring player is only about 30 years old, with another 50 years of his live ahead of him.

In basketball, the average career of a National Basketball Association (NBA) player is 6-7 seasons, with average salary of around $6.5 million per year. Again, the top players earn five times as much. For example, LeBron James salary was reportedly around $31 million during the 2016-2017 season.

The situation in professional baseball is very similar. Major League Baseball (MLB) players play on average for about 5 years. During their playing years in the MLB, they earn rather hefty salaries; the average is close to $3 million per year. As in the other professional sports, star players earn significantly more -- e.g., Clayton Kershaw earned around 32 million in 2016. The star athletes add significant amounts to their salaries from endorsements and commercials.

This picture is representative of all professional sports, including hockey, boxing, track and field, swimming, soccer and so on. Once they retire from their profession, their incomes fall off sharply in the non-athletic labor market they then find themselves. A professional athlete may have other skills that are marketable; after all, many have attended college. They may have studied physical education, sociology, engineering, etc. But their earnings as a high school coach or an engineer would be in the $40,000-$80,000 range, a fraction of their salaries as pro athletes, and that is assuming that the expertise they gained in college has been upgraded. To maintain their high standards of living that they get used to as pro athletes, they must rely on their savings and the income these savings generate. Although the high earnings of a short career offer the potential of a nice life after their sport career ends, many of them end up having relatively a modest standard of living. This is because they do not save enough and invest their funds properly and profitably. The tendency is to overestimate the length of their career and spend too much in relation to their expected lifetime earnings, to receive poor advice and to make poor investments. If one's living standard demands $500,000 per year (after adjusting for inflation of 2% per year), one needs an investment portfolio in excess of $12 million with this portfolio rising in value by around 2% per year to keep up with inflation.

Human Capital versus Other Assets

Some aspects of human capital that distinguishes it from most other assets is worth noting. First, human capital cannot be traded because of anti-slavery laws. However, the flow of the return from human capital, that is, the number of hours worked per unit of time, can and is sold and it is called "labor"; the person selling her or his <u>own</u> labor is paid a wage. While an owner of most other real asset, such as a house or piece of machinery, is separate from the asset itself, such is not the case for the owner of human capital; human capital is imbedded in oneself. The owner of a rental house located in Boston can be in Southern France enjoying the sun and the sea, living on the rent she receives. But civil engineer on a salary must be in location supervising the progress of the high-rise that is being built in Birmingham, Alabama, when the temperature stands at 100^0F and humidity is 100%.

Chapter 19

STOCK DIVIDENDS, STOCK SPLITS, AND STOCK BUYBACKS

Cash Dividends and Value of Stock

Let's say you own a small grocery store that is worth $85,000; this is the value of the store: its real estate, the shelves, the refrigerator, the lighting, the inventory, and the cash register – everything needed to run such a store. This is how much you could sell the store for. You also have a safe in which you keep the paperwork; you also have $300 in cash in the safe. You have no debt at all. So, if you wanted to sell the store including the safe and the cash in it you would get $85,300; the extra is for the $300 cash in the safe. Let's assume that the store and its contents are the only things you own in this world. Your net worth is $85,300. Tonight, as you are closing the shop you take $50 out of the safe and go to your rented room. How much is your net worth now? It is the $85,250 in the safe plus the $50 in your pocket; whether the $50 is kept in the safe or in your pocket does not change your net worth; it is still $85,300.

Instead of the store, what if you have shares in a company worth $85,300 and these shares are the only thing that you own? This figure represents your portion of how much this company is worth, and it includes the cash the company has in its bank accounts. The company decides to pay a dividend to its shareholders and your share turns out to be $300; you receive a check from the company for that amount. How much is your net worth now? Still $85,300. But something has changed: your shares are now worth $85,000 and you have $300 in cash. This means that a dividend reduces the value of a share by the amount of the dividend. You do actually observe this on the rare occasions when the overall market hardly moves and there is no particularly significant news that moves the specific stock in question.

So why do companies pay dividends at all? Well, not all companies pay dividends; Google has never paid a dividend since its inception. Some companies pay dividends because they always have in the past and their management feels that their shareholders expect to receive dividends. Especially for these companies, halting the payment of dividends may signal that the firm has financial problems. Some companies generate large amounts of cash but lack the opportunity to reinvest these funds in projects that offer returns that its shareholders expect to earn. If such a company has competent management that works for the benefit of its shareholders, it would not reinvest these funds in the company; the only economically efficient thing to do is to return these funds to its shareholders. In fact, if such a corporation invests these funds in low-return projects, the company and its stock lose value. Why? Suppose that you find a dozen companies that are similar in terms of riskiness and their stocks return around 12% per year. You select one and invest in its stock; a change in management causes the company to become less profitable but continues to invest in projects that return only 9%. Wouldn't you prefer taking cash out of the company and reinvest it in one of the other eleven similar companies? A good management would only invest in areas where it can earn "at least" 12%. That would help support the price of its shares.

Some investors argue that they need the dividends because it comprises a portion of their income. But nobody prevents these investors from selling some of their stock periodically to match what they would have received as dividend. It is this sort of argument that has led many companies to not pay dividends.

Stock Buybacks

Stock repurchase or *buyback* is another way to return cash to its stockholders that the company cannot invest in profitable projects. In recent years an increasing number of companies have elected to buy back their shares instead of paying dividends. The repurchasing of shares has the consequence of decreasing the number of shares outstanding. This means that future per share earnings and dividends rise. But there is no reason for the share price to change. The reason is that while the number of shares falls, the value of the company declines by the amount of cash used to buy back the shares; careful calculation shows that the decline in cash and the fall in the number of shares are such as to leave share value unchanged. One often hears the management of some companies claim that their shares are undervalued and buying back their stock is a good investment; this is pretty much nonsense. A more honest way of putting it is for management to say that "we have run out of sufficiently profitable investments and we are returning the excess cash to our shareholders is the right thing to do." Of course, putting this way can signal that the company or its management lacks good business opportunities.

Stock Dividend

Some companies instead of paying cash dividends pay *stock dividends*. There may be various reasons for this. One is that the company is not generating enough cash to use for various of its profitable projects and pay dividends too. Another reason might be that the business is not doing well enough and therefore needs all the cash it generates to stay afloat. For the shareholder, a stock dividend changes nothing in terms of the total value of her shareholding – she now has more shares, with each share worth less, just lower enough to leave the total value of her shareholding exactly as before.

Stock Split

Sometimes a company announces a *stock split*. This means that you wake up in the morning and learn that you have a larger number of shares than when you went to bed the night before. In a 3-for-1 stock split, each of your shares becomes 3 shares. But this doesn't mean that you are better or worse off than before the stock split. Think about it: you and your brother buy a house together, each owning one-half of it. To make things official you issue one share to each of you, for a total of 2 shares representing ownership in the house. Then one day the two of you decide that you should each own 2 shares in the house. How do you do it? By crossing the "one" on your shares and marking "two" on them. Has the value of the house or the value of your ownership in it changed? Not even by a cent; you have merely wasted your time and some ink. Take your $1 bill to the bank and exchange it for 4 quarters; are you better off? (This is another version of what economists call "money illusion").

So why do companies split their shares? It used to be that when the price of a stock rose too high, the company assumed that the high share price deterred investors from buying their stock. As investors and company managements have become more sophisticated in financial analysis they have come to understand that the "high" stock price does not prevent investment in their stock. Nowadays, with easy and inexpensive investment possibility through mutual funds, an expensive stock is not an obstacle. And we do observe really high prices for many stocks. Berkshire Hathaway Class A sells for around $300,000; Google shares are valued at around $1,200; Amazon stock is priced at about $1,800.

A dollar is a dollar –no matter how you cut it or paste it

Occasionally a company does what is referred to as *reverse stock split*. This happens when the share price of a company falls too low. So now your 3 shares become 1 share. A company may do a reverse stock split if the stock exchange on which it is listed sets a minimum price on the shares traded on that exchange. As with ordinary stock splits, your wealth is not affected by this change. It is said that when a server asked Yoggi Bera whether they should cut his 12" pizza into 4 or 6 slices, he told the server to cut it into 4 slices because he wasn't that hungry.

REFERENCES

Andolfatto, D. and Andrew Spewak, "Whither the Price of Bitcoin?," *Economic Synopses*, No. 1, 2019. https://doi.org/10.20955/es.2019.1

Akerloff, G. A., and R. J. Shiller. *Phishing for Phools*. (Princeton, NJ: Princeton University Press, 2015)

Berk, J., and P. DeMarzo. *Corporate Finance*. (Boston, MA: Pearson Education, 2014)

Bodie, Z., A. Kane, A.J. Marcus, and P. Mohanty. *Investments*. (New York, NY: McGraw-Hill Education, 2015)

Campbell, J.Y. *Financial Decisions and Markets*. (Princeton, NJ: Princeton University Press, 2018)

Duffie, D. *How Big Banks Fail and What to do About It*. (Princeton, NJ: Princeton University Press, 2011)

Fisher, I. *Theory of Interest*. (Philadelphia, PA: Porcupine Press, Inc., 1977)

Hull, J.C. *Options, Futures, and Other Derivatives*. (Boston, MA: Pearson Education, 2018)

Lo, Andrew W. Adaptative Markets. (Princeton, NJ: Princeton University Press, 2017)

Saunders, A., and Marcia M. Cornett. *Financial Market and Institutions*. (New York, NY: McGraw-Hill Education, 2015)

Shiller, R. J. *Irrational Exuberance.* (Princeton, NJ: Princeton University Press, 2015)

Taylor, A. M. *The Rat of Return on Everything*. NBER Reporter, National Bureau of Economic Research, No. 4, (December 2018), pp. 20-23.

Thaler, R. H. *The Winner's Curse.* (Princeton, NJ: Princeton University Press, 1992)

INDEX

Accounts Receivable	57
Adverse selection	25, 30
Agency problem	92
audit, 92	
Alpha, beta	86, 191
Amortization	66
fully amortized, 67	
Angel investor	194
Annuity	42
Antiques	147
Art work	149
Ask price	132
Assets	
financial, 52, 89	
liquid, 89	
nonfinancial, 52	
real, 89	
Athletes and other stars	205
Auction	
reservation price, 152	
reservation price as put option, 152	
winner's curse, 152	
Balance Sheet	58
Behavioral economics	34
Bid price	132
Blue sky laws	95
Bonds	77, 89, 127
bills, 130	
bonds, 127, 130	

Bonds (cont.)
   callable, 139
   collateral, 128
   collateralized, 129
   consol, 48, 137
   convertible, 139
   debenture, 131
   default, 128
   face value, 127
   interest, 127
   maturity, 127
   municipals, 140
   munis, 117
   notes, 130
   par value, 127
   price, 135, 137
   principal, 127, 133
   TIPS, 139
   unsecured, 131
   zero-coupon, 137
Buffett, Warren 117, 120
Business cycles 9
   phases, 14
Business sector
   stock performance, 116

CAPE (Shiller's) 107
Capital gain and loss 76
CAPM 87
Cash 52
   free, 60, 110
   one-period, 38

Cash (cont.)
    multiperiod, uniform, 42
    multiperiod, variable, 46

CDS	29
Certificate of Deposit, CD	78, 131
CFTC	94
Check cashing	32
Collateral	128
Collateralized security	129
Collectibles	146

    3-D printed art, 151
    antiques, 147
    art work, 149
    computer-generated, 151
    fake art, 149
    rare coins as precious metal, 154

Commercial banks	24

    bank run, 26

Common stock	100
Compound interest	43, 72
Comptroller of Currency	25
Consols	22
Consumer prices	

    CPI-U, 12
    CPI-W, 12
    PCE, 12

Consumer sentiment	109
Consumption	

    of goods, 50
    timing, 91

Convexity	136
Corporation	75

Corporation (cont.)
    agency problem, 92
    board of directors, 92
    separation of ownership, 92

Correlation	85
Cost of Capital	16
Cost, expense	56
Cost of goods sold	56
Counter party	167
Credit default swap, CDS	29, 179
Credit union	27
Crowd funding	194
Currency	89
Cryptocurrency	157

    Bitcoin, 157

Current Assets	58
Current Liabilities	58
Day trading	124
Default	128
Defensive stocks	14
Deficit	18
Deflation	14
Depository institution	24
Depreciation	56
Derivatives	89
Dice, rolling	36
Discount factor	40
Discount rate	40, 44
Discounting formula	45
Diversification	84

    benefits, 85

Diversified portfolio	121
Dividends	69, 75, 173
cash, 209	
yield, 75	
Dodd-Frank	95
Dollar-cost averaging	122
Earnings per share, EPS	59, 60
Economic sectors	6
Economist, The	14
Efficient Market Hypothesis	
efficient markets, 33	
EMH, 34	
Exchange traded fund, ETF	185
bid-ask spread, 188	
margin buying, 187	
short sale, 187	
tax, 188	
Expense	56
Fannie Mae	11
FASB	61
Federal Deposit Insurance, FDIC	26, 74
Federal Reserve Districts	21
Federal Reserve System, the Fed	21, 22
FOMC, 23	
reserves, 22	
Finance companies	28
Financial accounting	55
Financial institutions	18
Financial intermediaries	18
Financial markets	18

FINRA	95
Forwards, Futures	177
forwards, 177	
futures, 178	
Freddie Mac	11
FSOC	95
Fundamental analysis	106
Future value	38
*G*AAP	61
GDP composition	6
Going public	31
Great Depression	102
Great Recession	10, 103
Gross Domestic Product	1
Canada, China, 4	
EU, Japan, Mexico, 4	
composition, 6	
real GDP, 3	
sectors, 6	
Growth stocks	113
*H*edge fund	190
Human Capital	63, 200
compared to other assets, 208	
education, 203	
lifetime earnings profile, 202	
Hyperinflation	155
*I*ASB	61
Illegal activity	2
Imputed rent	2
Income Statement	56

Income	49
Inflation	14
Initial public offering, IPO	19, 31

Insurance
    term life, 29
    universal life, 29
    whole life, 29

Interest rate
    compound, 70, 72
    forward, 179
    futures, 179
    long term, 77
    negative, 70
    simple, 72
    short term, 77
    spot, 179
    zero-lower bound, 71

Investing
    active, 185
    day trading, 125
    dollar-cost averaging, 122
    margins, 123, 187
    mechanisms, 122
    passive, 184
    regret, 122
    sector investing, 184
    shorting, 123, 187
    secondary, 19

Investment banks	30
Investment companies	19
Investment return	73
Irrational exuberance	107

IRS	21
*J*anuary effect	105
*K*ahneman	35
*L*everage	63, 123
Liabilities	58
Liquidity, assets	89
Listed stocks	99
Loan	77
Loan sharks	32
LTCM	174
*M*argin transactions	123, 187
Market makers	97
Market mispricing	174

Markets
   capital market, 20
   money market, 20
   primary, 19
   Secondary, 20

Maturity, bond	127
Mechanics of investing	120
Mehrain, Mehrdad	119
Mergers and acquisitions (M&A)	31
Momentum	109
Money market mutual fund	189
Moral hazard	25, 30
Mortgage as annuity	48
Munger, Charlie	120
Mutual funds	184

   closed-end, 188
   net asset value (NAV), 183

Mutual funds (cont.)
    open-end (MuF), 183
    sector investing, 184

Mutual organizations   23

*N*ational Credit Union Adm (NCUA)   28

NBER   117

Net Income   56

*O*ptions   166
    American, 168
    Black-Scholes formula, 174
    calls, 168
    counterparty, 167
    creation of options, 168
    European, 168
    exercise or strike price, 168
    expiration, 168
    premium, 168, 172
    properties, 172
    put-call parity, 173
    put options, 168
    write or sell, 168
    zero-sum game, 170

Outgo   50

Outstanding forecasters   117

*P*EG   115

Pensions
    401k plans, 196
    defined benefit, 195
    defined contribution, 164
    ERISA, 196
    PBGC, 196

Pensions (cont.)
    pay-as-you-go, 196
Perpetuity   48
Ponzi and pyramids   197
Portfolio
    diversified, 121
    "right" stocks to buy, 120
Precious metals   154
Predictability of stock prices   104
Preferred stock   100
Present value (PV)   38, 42
Price-earnings ratio (P/E)   60, 107, 112
    forward P/E, 113
    PEG, 115
    trailing, 113
Principal   66, 67, 72
Private equity   192
Proforma statement   61
Purchasing power parity (PPP)   5
Put as price guarantee   152

Rate of interest   38
Rate of return   38, 69, 74
Real estate investment trust (REIT)   189
Real estate   159
    Chicago home prices, 161
    return on housing, 163
    San Francisco home prices, 161
    stocks and housing returns, 163
Regret (investment)   122
Reservation price as put option/guarantee   152, 128
Reserves   22

Retained earnings	56
Return and inflation	141
Return on investment	73
Return t0 stocks	101
Reverse swap	181
Risk and return	79
Risk	41, 80
aversion, 80	
compensation for, 84	
diversifiable, 81	
idiosyncratic, 81	
known, 80	
market, 81	
specific, 81	
types, 81	
undiversifiable, 81	
unknown, 80	
volatility, 103	
Run on banks	26
Savings and Loan (S&L)	27
Savings institutions	26
Savings	50
SEC regulation	31
Securities Act of 1933, 94	
Securities Exchange Act, 94	
Securities	89
Securities firms	30
Securities Exchange Commission (SEC)	31
Separation of management/ownership	92

Shares	96
Shareholder	75, 96
Shorts and shorting	124
SIPC	94
Size of the US economy	4
Spending	50
Standard deviation and risk	111
Startup	82
Stockholder	75
Stockholder equity	58
Stock market indexes	98

    Dow-Jones (DJIA), 83
    Nasdaq, 83
    NYSE, 83
    S&P 500, 83
    Wilshire 5000, 84

Stocks	89

    buybacks, 211
    cash dividends, 209
    common, 100
    cumulative preferred, 100
    market, 98
    market maker, 97
    price predictability, 104
    preferred, 100
    return to stocks, 101
    reverse split, 214
    split, 212
    stock dividend, 212
    terminal value, 110
    timing, 106
    valuation, 109

Stocks (cont.)
    volatility, 103
Street name   124
Swaps   181

*T*echnical analysis   104
    technician, 104
The Fed and swaps   181
Time deposit   69
Time preference   37
Too big to fail   12
Total assets, total liabilities   58
Total return   101

*U*ncertainty   81
Underground economy   3
Unit investment trust   190
US Treasury Department   20
    IRS, 20
Usury   32

*V*enture capital   193
Volatility   103, 172

*W*arrants   176
Wealth   51
Winner's curse   152

*Y*ield
    inverted, 145
    yield curve, 144

Zeros (bonds) 137

www.ingramcontent.com/pod-product-compliance
Lightning Source LLC
Chambersburg PA
CBHW021812170526
45157CB00007B/2555